#IWILL

DEVOTIONAL
52 WEEKS OF INSPIRATION

CHIDI WOSU
I Will ENspire Publications

DEDICATED TO

To Momma and Papa Wosu

Thank you for being the best parents a girl can ever dream of. Thank you for being my biggest cheerleaders

To my siblings

Eliada, HeCareth, and Emi you guys are more than siblings, you are my best friends

To my friends turned into family

You all are the best motivators a girl can have

CONTENTS

INTRODUCTION

Let's be honest, the struggle is real. Nothing will exempt you from facing challenges and difficulties in life. However, the fabric of a human being has little to do with the challenges they face, but more about who they become through what they have overcome. Failure is just a lesson in achieving one's next victory. At the end of some of the hardest races run, is a victory that cannot be quantified.

If you are reading this, you might be looking for encouragement, insight, or just a different perspective. The goal of this book is to help you find morsels of encouragement through God's word, making it relevant and applicable to the situations we face today.

My ultimate hope, is that you would walk away from this book understanding yourself and God more. My prayer is that after getting through this devotional book this year, that you would have a better knowledge of understanding yourself and why God put you on this earth.

Through pain one can find their purpose. Through misery one can find their ministry. Through calamity one can find their calling. Every tear, every sleepless lonely night, every traumatic experience in life is worth it if you use that pain towards your destiny in life. You were fearfully and wonderfully made. You are the handwork of God himself. You can and you WILL do all things through Christ who strengthens you.

WEEK 1

Even Steak Can Look Like Dog Food

"Do not give dogs what is sacred; do not throw your pearls to pigs. If you do, they may trample them under their feet, and then turn and tear you to pieces."

Matthew 7:6

Coal and Diamonds are made of the same element of carbon. The only difference is that it takes a lot more time and pressure to make a diamond than it does a lump of coal.

There is a blessing that God has in store for you. People may look at you, and just see a lump of coal, they don't see the diamond that is forming under the surface. Therefore, it is so important to check who you are giving information that God had delivered to you Himself. You cannot tell everyone because not everyone will see it through God's eyes. Remember that even steak can be mistaken for dog food.

Meaning people can take something sacred and cheapen it by their lack of understanding. This can be dangerous because people can make you stop having faith in something God has told you.

God has given you a word. Something that is so special and is just for you. It might be a word about your purpose, it might be a word about what God wants you to do, or even what God is about to give you. When God gives you something so sacred you must be careful with it. Why? Because you have an enemy who is always trying to make the sacred seem cheap. You have someone seeking to devour all that God has in store for you.

Take some time to meditate on the word that God has given you. Maybe you told your best friend and they told you that was crazy. Maybe you told your family and they didn't understand, however, God understands. God knows, and He doesn't want you giving your special gift that He gave you to someone who understands not, and cares less.

WEEK 2

A Closed Mouth Don't Get Fed

"Ask and it will be given to you; seek and you will find; knock and the door will be opened to you."

Matthew 7:7

God has blessed me to be able to fly to different parts of America. During one of my travels, my layover flight landed at the Atlanta International Airport. I was starving, so I went to the nearby restaurant for some bacon cheese fries. I guess great minds think alike because the man in front of me ordered the same dish. The cashier took the order and then asked the man to move down the line so that the line cook could make his order. Usually, when you reached the place where the cook was, upon her looking at you, you reiterated the order that you had just given to the cashier. It seems repetitive, but without doing this, you would not receive food.

The man must have had no knowledge of this, and just stared at the woman wondering where his fries were. The female cook then asked,

"What was your order sir?"

He replied, "I ordered fries ma'am!"

She then replied, "Well what type of fries' sir? We have many kinds, you've got to tell me exactly what you want!"

He replied, "Well I told the cashier what I wanted!"

She then said, "Well you have to tell me! I'm the cook! You've got to say your order, cause a closed mouth don't get fed!"

At this point, I screamed out in laughter. I love Atlanta.

If you want a blessing from God, you must ask. You cannot approach Jesus, and just think He is going to give you what you've been desiring if you never bothered to ask. Just like the restaurant, you need to ask, before you receive. Also, you need to be specific with your request. Tell God exactly what you want! Although God knows the desire of your heart, just like the restaurant staff knows you desired food, you still must order before you are given anything!

Secondly, know what restaurant you are going to. You can't go to a burger joint and order pasta. This means you should know that you can't ask God for things that are OBVIOUSLY not in His best interest for you and expect Him to do them. Don't ask for someone else's husband, because the answer is no. Don't ask to steal someone's job because that is not in God best interest for you. You are going to the King God to ask Him for His will for you. The key word here is *His will*. Going to say, just because God doesn't give you exactly what you requested, doesn't mean He can't bless you with something that is equivalent or better than what you asked for.

Back to the restaurant, sometimes you must ask more than once, to receive what you have asked for. Sometimes you must pray without ceasing until God answers your prayers.

Always ask to be in His will. Make your request known, but know this, a bad day in God's will is better than a good day in your own!

In addition, stop telling the wrong people what you want. Stop venting to your friends about the type of relationship you want, or the type of job you want. Tell Jesus! God is the only one that is going to be able to help you with that problem.

Just because you asked, and God said no, does not mean you did not receive an answer, it means that God said no, or not now. Receive your answer, and take it as a blessing. Pray that God helps you to align your desires with His will for you so that you won't always be praying for the wrong things for yourself.

It never hurts to ask, but be open to when the will of God differs from your own. It might not be exactly what you asked for, and it might end up seemingly costing more, but the benefits are so much greater.

WEEK 3

Not To The Swift Or The Strong

"I have seen something else under the sun: The race is not to the swift or the battle to the strong, nor does food come to the wise or wealth to the brilliant or favor to the learned; but time and chance happen to them all."

Ecclesiastics 9:11

The other day I was watching a documentary about animals. As some of you already know, lions are separated into tribes called prides. There was one pride that was very small. Not to mention that their hunting ground was not in the best area. At that point the narrator said,

"Yet success is not just governed by where they live and what the changing seasons bring, but survival comes just as much from their ability to defend what is theirs…."

Your personal success has nothing to do with where you come from, but it has everything to do with the God you serve and how willing and ready you are to fight for what God has promised you. Yes, it is true, changing seasons will bring about different battles. Like the lions, because of the place they lived, they did not have much food, so they had to share the little that they had. However, when the dry season came, because they knew how to live in desolate areas, they could easily survive, while those prides that lived in more prosperous areas suffered.

Just like the narrator said, your success has nothing to do with where you came from, who you are, or what is currently happening to you right now. It all depends on your ability to defend yourself from an enemy who is basically coming to devour your blessing! How do you do this? You need to learn how to pray defensively. Pray when blessings come, and pray against assignments that the enemy might have against you. But now you might ask, how about if I have been praying and I continue to get attacked?

Sometimes God takes you through a difficult season to make you a stronger person. Think of a time when you went through a hard season that God brought you out of. Did it not make your view on life change? Did it not make your faith to graduate from the level it had previously been? You need to know that sometimes God takes you through something to get you to something. Sometimes God will put you through a struggle because He knows that in the next season, you will need the strength that your current season will provide for you. The next season is coming, and although you will be done with the past challenges, you need to get ready for the future ones. The race is not to the swift or battle to the strong, it's just to the one who perseveres! Maybe you've been running a long race, maybe your muscles are tired. Well aren't you glad, that you are not running this race alone, and when you get tired, God is there to take the baton and help you to finish the race. God is there with Gatorade on hand when you are spiritually thirsty. He is there to quieten your spirit when it seems you have lost.

Sometimes your struggle can end up being your blessing. Maybe you don't have a lot of money right now, but that will make you more resourceful with what you have. Maybe you're not good in a subject, well, that will teach you how to teach others that subject when they do not understand. No matter what the problem is, your struggle can become your biggest resource in the future.

Remember that just like the lions, the race isn't to the person with the best situation, the prettiest, the most handsome person, or the person with the most accolades, but it is to the one who endures to the end!

So fight for what God promised you! Fight for it! Tell the devil he is a liar and defend with your whole being what is yours!

WEEK 4

Arrival and Departure

"Trust in the Lord with all your heart and lean not on your own understanding; in all your ways submit to him, and he will make your paths straight."

Proverbs 3:5-6

I was sitting in the airport, and God started to show me several connections between the symbols at the airport and life. To get to your destination, you must leave where you are to get to where you are going. There must be a departure before there is an arrival.

God was showing me that, for you to get to the will of God in your life, there are some things that you are going to have to depart from. There are some friends you must leave, there are some places you must stop going, and there are some habits that you are going to have to reform.

Many people tend to believe you can get to know God on a deeper level, without letting go of some things in your life. However, that is a lie. If you want to get to know God in a new way, it may take you letting some things go.

Now in departing from the things you can feel one of two ways. You can be very anxious and want to leave your current situation very badly, or you can be scared and resist leaving. You might be afraid of the one thing that is going to get you to your destiny. You may fear planes, but that is the thing that will help you reach your height. You may be afraid to take that bold step. People might tell you that it doesn't make sense, or that you will fail, however, if God is for you, who can be against you? (Romans 8:31)

For the people who are anxious to go, your flight may be 'delayed'. Meaning God is forcing you to stay in the same spot for your own safety. You don't want to get on that plane with a storm brewing over you. You don't want to get into that relationship prematurely. You don't want to get that job and later hate it! God is 'delaying your flight' so He can make sure the conditions are right! The bible says, "Trust in the Lord with all your heart and lean not on your own understanding; in all your ways submit to Him, and He will make your paths straight." (Proverbs 3:5-6)

He will make everything straight! You might want to leave your current situation right now, but God might be telling you to stay, and on the other hand, you might be hesitant to go, and God is pushing you out of the airport. Just obey Him, and listen to what God is telling you.

Some of you feel that you don't have what it takes to depart from your current situation. You may think, how can I do great things with the amount of money or obstacles that I have, being that I'm not rich or successful. Yes, you might not have the money to get into a business class like some other people. Your journey to your destination might not be that smooth. It might not be as comfortable as other peoples'. Some people will leave their current destination and walk straight into first class. Their journey will be easy. However, your journey might not take the same path. You may be surrounded by people that make it hard for you to find rest while you are on the plane! You may be uncomfortable, and you may have distractions, but that doesn't mean you're on the wrong flight! God knows what He is doing, and the devil will try to make you feel you are in the wrong spot. Knows this, it doesn't matter which way you get there if you obey God and move, God will get you to the destination where you need to be!

WEEK 5

When The Snow Won't Melt

Ecclesiastes 3:1-8

During the winter on the east coast, some places get hit with tragic amounts of snow. I remember one year it snowed so bad that heaps of snow taller than cars flooded parking lots and streets. I even heard a woman say, "It seems like this snow is never going to melt! I almost can't imagine it being summer."

This reminded me of when we face difficult seasons in our lives. Sometimes these seasons can tend to last forever. It can seem like winter is never going to end, and the heaps of snow, aka, the problems in your life, are never going to melt away. It can also seem like you are stuck. Some of you that have driven in the snow, know that if the snow gets too high, and you try to drive in it without shoveling some of it, you will get stuck. Life can be similar to this in that, we have seasons in which we are pushing and yet we feel like we are not moving forward.

As I looked at these snow mounds, some of which were bigger than me, I thought about the characteristics of snow. Snow is the most silent natural disaster one can experience. You can go to sleep one night and wake up in the middle of a blizzard. Sometimes, problems come upon us all suddenly. "Everything was fine until yesterday," are things that start to cloud our minds. I started to think, is there anything good that comes from snow?

Well if you didn't know, snow actually reflects heat, it gives off energy into the atmosphere, when the sun shines upon it. When we grow cold, when it seems we have no strength, when God shines upon us, we produce something useful. Realize that sometimes God is creating heaps of snow around you so that you can use those problems as your ministry. Maybe God wants you to use this problem to encourage others on how to cope. God is trying to make you a better person! He is trying to make you stronger, and you need some 'cold times' to do that. Some of the testimonies you have had could not have been if God didn't let a little bit of snow fall.

Also, I noticed that when the snow first fell, people stayed in their homes and they didn't dare to go outside. Sometimes when problems come, the first thing we do is run for cover. We pray that God will just take it away! But God isn't always going to take our problems immediately away because there is always a blessing in the midst of every problem. There is always a lily in the valley. Meaning that even in the midst of a horrible situation there is always a lesson that can be gained from it. It's our duty to figure out what that lesson is and learn how to cope and deal with the card we are dealt with. But find encouragement in knowing that God will never give you any more than you can handle.

As it kept snowing, and people realized that the snow wasn't going anywhere, they learned to maneuver through it. It got to the point that 5 inches of snow wasn't alarming because people had seen much worse.

Now I know some of you have been through some situations in your life, where you thought, it could be worse, because you had been through worse! You have been through 2 feet, so 5 inches was like dust to you. That's how God is trying to make you. He is trying to teach you perfect faith. Meaning that 2 feet can fall, and you are not shaken or stirred because you know that God will get you through!

The snow will make you stronger. Trials will come, and troubles will seem like they will overtake you, however, you have God on your side, you will be able to dare what seems like massive problems. Know that if some snow didn't fall in the winter, you wouldn't be so thankful when summer time came. Meaning that if bad things didn't happen, you wouldn't be so thankful when good things appeared.

Ecclesiastes 3:1-8 describes that to everything there is a season and a time for every purpose under heaven. Right now you may be stuck in a season that doesn't seem like it is ever going to end, but seasons change. Joy will come! Take heart, God is just trying to make you stronger, because next winter will come, and the snow might be deeper. However, because you've learned how to trudge yourself through the snow during this season, it won't overcome you.

Trust in God, and He will make things make sense even when they don't. He will give you that hot cup of cocoa when you are stuck. God will give you a little sprinkle of sunshine, even in the midst of your winter season! Trust in Him and He will give you strength to get through.

WEEK 6

Platinum Power

"Endure hardship as discipline; God is treating you as his children. For what children are not disciplined by their father?"

Hebrews 12:9

Life can get real, and when life gets real you can start thinking the God has abandoned you. Bad things happen to the best of us, and it can leave us worn out and make us lose faith. The death of a loved one, the loss of a relationship, even a drastic downward change in status can make us think that God is angry at us. We may even start to think that God doesn't love us and that he is punishing us for something that we have done wrong.

I used to know someone who often went through very difficult, painful experiences in her life. It seemed that every time she was getting over one blow, another one would come to quickly throw her off track. She began to think God was mad at her. This was when I had to explain to her what platinum purpose is.

Let's talk about platinum, shall we?

Platinum is a rare precious metal only composing of about .003% of the earth crust. It is used to make very expensive jewelry and is a more precious metal than gold or silver. One thing about platinum is that it only melts at over 3000 degrees. And it only gives off its best properties after it has been under fire, melted, and reconstructed.

The first thing you should know is that if you are going through a difficult situation right now, it is not because God hates you, it's because He knows how much you're worth and He is putting you through this season so that you can become pure. Sometimes, in order for us to shed some of the bad qualities we have, we must be put through the fire. But here is a point to remember, the more precious the metal, the hotter the fire needs to be in order for purification to result.

Meaning, if you are going through a lot more than your gold and copper friends, it's probably because you have a platinum purpose! Do not compare your hardships to others. Just like the Bible verse says, these hardships teach us discipline. It may be a tough season now, but you will be surprised how the season ends up helping you get through something else in the long run.

Platinum purposes are rare. Not everyone is going to be able to endure the heat that God might put you under. Why does God put you through such intense heat? Because He knows that your best qualities will not shine through unless He does this to you.

Only God can infuse that type of power in a person, but that power will come with trials you have to endure. The goal is to remember that although you have trouble on every side, God has not forsaken you. Remember Job? The only reason why Job went through so much is because God was so happy with Him, and He knew that Job would not forsake Him. God knew He could put Job through the fire, and he would come out shining!

You will have to go through the platinum process in order to get the platinum power. Don't despise the process, just pray that God helps you get through it in one piece.

WEEK 7

Be Anxious FOR NOTHING

"Do not be anxious about anything, but in every situation, by prayer and petition, with thanksgiving, present your requests to God."

Philippians 4:6

What does the word anxious mean? Anxious can be taken from many words. Looking at the etymology, it is taken from a Latin word meaning an uneasy and troubled mind. It is also taken from the word "angere" which means to choke or to cause distress. Also, we can look at the word "tjeskoba" meaning tightness or narrowness. Anxiousness also can mean the strong earnest desire to want something.

In life, we approach many situations that can make us anxious. It's funny how anxiousness, like the etymology, can make us uneasy and can trouble our thoughts. Anxiousness can choke you from being happy in the state that you're in and can narrow your mindset as to the plethora of options that God can lay out for you. It can also narrow your mindset as to how powerful the God you serve is. It is no wonder that God tells us to be anxious for nothing! It does not merit you much to be stressed out over problems that you cannot fix. Then what should we do? Well, that's where the rest of the verse comes in.

Prayer and supplication are not the same thing. Prayer is actually communicating with God. It is telling God how you feel, thanking Him for who He is, and just having a conversation with God. Supplication is actually making a request to God. It is a certain type of prayer. All of your prayer language to God should not ONLY be supplication. Think about it like this, how would you feel if you had a friend that only called you when they needed something? God wants to hear from you all the time, every day. He wants to talk to you, see what's up with you and see how you're feeling. He also wants you to lay out your requests before him instead of worrying about it and putting it on yourself.

Finally, the verse said prayer and supplication, with thanksgiving. This means that you are thanking God for blessing you already. Not just blessing you with what you are currently asking for, but blessing you with the things that he has blessed you with in the past. It's being thankful for the things God will do and has done for you.

I traveled to my hometown New Orleans to watch the Super bowl in my city. We went to a friend's house for a Superbowl party. In the second quarter, the Saints were down by a couple of points, and everyone was feeling the anxiety. All of the sudden, someone said, "Let's put on some music! The Saints got to the Superbowl didn't they?" At that point, everyone started dancing. They started dancing like we had already won. I overheard an older woman talking, and she said that New Orleans had really put itself together after Katrina, and the Saints making it to the Superbowl was just a testament to the strong spirit of the city. All through the weekend, you would hear fans say, "Win or lose, we are still having the Saints parade on Tuesday!"

This goes to show, we can thank God before we win the game, because we actually made it to the game! You might not be done with the race in your life yet, but you are not in the same place you were last year, and that is reason enough to thank God. It is also reason enough to thank God that He has the ability to make a way out of no way for your current situation!

I know it's hard. I know you want it so bad, but you've got to get into a mindset of giving whatever situation to God and not letting it stress you out. Take heart, whatever the outcome, God is not in the business of abandoning you and He will surely take care of you.

WEEK 8

Foggy Roads

"Trust in the Lord with all your heart and lean not on your own understanding; in all your ways submit to him, and he will make your paths straight."

Proverbs 3: 5-6

When I started my new job, the hefty commute had me wake up at about 5:00 AM to arrive at work at 7:00 AM. If it wasn't hard enough to get out of bed, I had an hour in the car to drive the monotonous scenic route of the Delaware Valley. One morning, I remember the fog was so heavy. The fog was so thick that I could only see about two feet in front of me. I slowed the car down in order to maintain control. In driving school, when I was younger, I remember my brother gave me a tip that I would use for the rest of my driving life. "When you can't see in front of you, use the line as your guide. Even if you can't see in front of you if you use the line you will never drift off the road." Here I was, eyes still heavy with sleep, following the line for my dear life so that I would know what direction to go.

God sometimes puts us in situations where we cannot see what is in front of us. Luckily in His word, God gave us a "line" to follow so that we will not stumble. Proverbs 3:5-6 states that you should trust the Lord with all your heart. What exactly does that mean? How is trust actually defined? Trust can be synonymic with the words confidence, faith, reliance, and belief. Trust is full reliance and dependence on something else. It can be for numerous things, but usually, trust is based on a promise of something to be fulfilled—even if one is not 100% sure how that promise will take place.

Trust is putting all faith in God to handle a situation although you don't know all the answers. Trust is finding peace in not knowing all the answers and relinquishing all authority of a situation to Christ. Trust is the hope that faith thrives upon. In looking at the metaphor of driving to a destination, God often times lets us know, even if it is vague, what the end of the story will be. God will give us a bird's eye view sometimes of where He wants you to be, but He might not give you all the details.

Why doesn't God answer all your questions? God is all about the journey. We live in a society where fast answers are the norm. God is all about taking his children through a journey in order to develop them. Also, God doesn't answer all your questions because if He did, you would have no need to strengthen your faith, self-control, trust, and other fruits of the spirit. Ultimately, God needs HIS name to be praised. Because of this, He doesn't answer all of your questions so that you can properly develop into the person God has so much purposed you to be.

The key is even though you can't see in front of you, God gives you a line to follow and this is His word. All we have to do is follow Him and trust Him that that "line" will take us to our destination. Trust God to the extent that even if we look around and see nothing, that we know that God is directing us to a place where he needs us to be.

Trusting in God is fully contingent upon letting go of what you thought you knew without knowing what will happen. It is the process of learning how to be okay with unanswered questions and the embodiment of realizing that whatever happens, whether you wanted it to happen or not if you are in God's perfect will, it is much better than anything you could have planned for yourself. Trust is blind but so necessary in order for us to experience true peace and joy unspeakable.

WEEK 9

Key Chains

"But those who hope in the Lord will renew their strength. They will soar on wings like eagles; they will run and not grow weary, they will walk and not be faint."

Isaiah 40:31

As a standard process for the mechanic I take my car to, they ask for your keys so that they can move the car about as needed. I entrusted the keys of my car into the care of the mechanics as I went about my day. Upon coming back to the mechanic, my key chain had completely unraveled, leaving me with a handful of keys. In an effort to keep my keys intact, I rummaged through my belongings to try to find an extra key chain.

While I was looking for the extra key chain, I recollected all the key chains I had thrown away over the year, regretting the fact I had tossed them aside, and thinking that I had missed out. How many times does something that you did not expect fall apart? How many times do we go through unexpected heartbreak and all we have left are the pieces of what once was whole? A marriage that held a family together is suddenly ripped to shreds, a relationship headed towards the aisle suddenly ends, and life around you seems to be in shambles.

I relate this to my keychain because there was nothing wrong with my key ring. It was completely intact. Then, without warning, it became useless. How many times do we lose something sacred to us in life, and we begin to think of all of our "missed opportunities?" We go through our minds trying to figure out the "should haves, could haves, and would haves." However, God does not want us to live a life of regret. He tells us in His word to forget the past and to focus on what is new and in front of you (Isaiah 43: 18-19). We have to get away from regretting our past, and look to the future of hope! Even if the keychain unraveled, or something that we didn't expect falls apart, we can't think of the things that have come and gone. We have to set our sights on the new thing that God has in store for us.

When I finally stopped trying to find a key chain in my house, I remember I was going home for the holidays. Surely my mom had a spare keychain hidden in the house somewhere. I would just have to wait a couple of weeks. The thing about God's blessings is, you will often times have to wait. However, you can be sure that the day will come, even though you do have to wait. In the wait, God will hold you together, just like I found a temporary solution to hold my keys together. The Bible says "But those who hope in the Lord will renew their strength. They will soar on wings like eagles; they will run and not grow weary, they will walk and not be faint." (Isaiah 40:31)

So I patiently waited until I got home. I had ordered a bag a month prior to me losing my key chain. I asked my mother for the package, which was shipped to her home instead of my own since I knew I was coming home for the holidays. Immediately she handed me the box that had inside of it a beautiful leather bag. I had completely let go of the key ring situation, knowing that I would find one in due time. I started to investigate the bag and look at the different aspects, and my eye came across a part of the bag that I left unwrapped. I unwrapped it slowly to find a beautiful designer key chain, with a strong stainless steel ring. I couldn't believe it! It came and I didn't even expect it.

Firstly, like my keychain, God will give you something way better than what you have lost. Secondly, God sometimes takes you through wilderness situations, so that when He does give you that keychain, or that blessing, you are all the more appreciative of it. Thirdly, God knows what's going to happen before it happens. Meaning God knew my keychain would unravel, so he provided another even before I lost the initial key chain. God is already putting things in the works for you if you have lost something. He is already setting things in your favor. All you have to do is wait!

WEEK 10

Bad Habits

"Even now, declares the Lord, return to me with all your heart, with fasting and weeping and mourning. Rend your heart and not your garments. Return to the Lord your God, for he is gracious and compassionate, slow to anger and abounding in love, and he relents from sending calamity."

Joel 2:12-13

I was watching the History Channel about the history of crack and cocaine. Cocaine has an amazing history, being that it was used as a cure-all remedy for headaches, colds, and even schizophrenia. An interesting point to note is that after the Civil War in the US, many people who were injured became addicted to morphine, and opium, which was used to relieve the pain. Cocaine during this time was used to "wean" people off morphine and opium.

This reminds me of what we sometimes do when we are hurting. We will end a bad relationship and quickly look for a replacement to cure our loneliness. We will pour ourselves into one thing to stop the pain we feel from being cut off from another thing. What we do not realize is that if what we run to is not God, we can be connecting ourselves with an even more painful addiction that can be harder to break.

This is very true in relationships. One love affair will end, and we are ready to be with someone new, not at all thinking that Mr. or Ms. New will come with new problems. We go broke, spending money on things to make us happy. Even try to find joy in our careers, working ourselves to a pulp to try to wean ourselves of the sadness that we are currently experiencing. The saddest thing is just like cocaine, they will wean you off of the addiction that you had, however, they will start a brand new one if you are dependent upon them for your happiness. For instance, if you always work out when you are feeling down, and one day you cannot work out, what are you going to do? That is why it is so important for us to lean on Jesus when we have been cut off from something we were so attached to. He is the only one who can take the pain away.

This is what people used to do in the Bible. When they were in terrible anguish they would physically rip their clothes, which was said to make people feel a bit better about the incident. However, God said, rend your hearts! Meaning, bring to Him the stuff that makes you cry, and the issues you face daily. Turn to Him with your weeping, and with your loneliness. He is the only one that can cure your pain. Nothing else, or nobody else can.

WEEK 11

Don't Let Go!

"When the man saw that he could not overpower him, he touched the socket of Jacob's hip so that his hip was wrenched as he wrestled with the man. Then the man said, "Let me go, for it is daybreak." But Jacob replied, "I will not let you go unless you bless me." The man asked him, "What is your name?" "Jacob," he answered. Then the man said, "Your name will no longer be Jacob, but Israel, because you have struggled with God and with humans and have overcome." Jacob said, "Please tell me your name." But he replied, "Why do you ask my name?" Then he blessed him there. So Jacob called the place Peniel, saying, "It is because I saw God face to face, and yet my life was spared." The sun rose above him as he passed Peniel, and he was limping because of his hip."

Genesis 32: 25-31

Many Christians know the saying that goes, "Pray Until Something Happens, " or P.U.S.H. Prayer is your direct communication with God, however, it is also a way for you to combat what the enemy is trying to accomplish. Prayer is powerful because even at the last minute it can change things. P.U.S.H praying is aggressive praying. It is not growing weary until results occur.

Sometimes, blessings are not just going to be thrown into your lap. Why? Because the devil is out there trying to steal the things that God has meant for you. I think of the blessings I have missed out on, not because they were not meant for me, and not because I didn't ask, but mainly because I didn't use the power of prayer, and faith in action to fight the devil when he tried to steal from me.

In the story of Jacob, we see a man that wants so desperately to be blessed. He wants to be blessed so much that he actually wrestled the "Man" or what in some text is called an angel. The first point to consider is sometimes you are going to have to wrestle with men in order for you to get the blessing that God has in store for you! Sometimes you are going to have to go to that office twice, or send more than one email, or get rejected at least once in order for you to finally receive your true blessing.

For example. I knew someone who really wanted to apply to a particular graduate school. At first, she was discouraged because it had a high ranking and she didn't think she would be able to compete. However, God told her to apply anyway. She was obedient and went to apply, but she could not pay the application fee. She went to ask for a fee waiver and she was rejected by a one liner email. At this point, she could have given up, however, she decided that if God told her that she was to apply to this school He would make a way. She asked the woman again, if she could have an application waiver. The woman said no, and this time was becoming irate. At this point, the girl prayed and wrote one more email. She made a conviction in her mind that she would just keep asking until the woman said yes. Guess what, in that third email, the woman finally relented, giving her almost $300.00 for an application waiver! Sometimes you got to keep pushing and be persistent. Be prayerful, and realize it's not over until God says it's over.

The second point to consider is as he was wrestling the man, his hip socket got knocked out of place. It is true that when we are believing God for something and pressing toward the mark, and making accomplishments, the devil will place events in our lives that will knock us right off our feet. He will make you sick in the midst of finals. He will let that relationship end right when that deadline is approaching. Your hip socket will get knocked out, but that doesn't mean that you should stop pressing toward you blessing!

The man said, to let him go because daybreak was coming. Some situations you will want to let go because it seems that the battle is already lost. It seems your blessing is so far gone, that there is no way that you will be able to attain it from this situation. However, that is when you need to hold on a little tighter. That is when Jacob said, I won't let you go until you bless me! Don't let your blessing go! Have faith that it is going to happen. If God has promised you something, hold on to it! It will come to pass.

Jacob might have walked away from wrestling with the man with a limp, however, Jacob walked away with his blessing in hand. Going to say, yeah, your pride might be a little hurt, however, if you persevere, to the end, you will get your blessing! The text says the sun rose on Jacob, and Jacob had received his blessing. Your hip socket might be knocked out right now, but do not let go! Your blessing is well on its way!

WEEK 12

You Can Win

"I have seen something else under the sun: The race is not to the swift or the battle to the strong, nor does food come to the wise or wealth to the brilliant or favor to the learned; but time and chance happen to them all."

Ecclesiastics 9:11

One night I watched one of the wildcard games for the playoffs for football. One of the teams was losing for the entire game, even into the 3rd half! It looked like it was over, like there was no hope for them. Surely with a score of 31 to 10, they would never be able to come back. It was too late. I watched as the commentators made references to the game going to the team that was at the moment winning. However, something struck me about the losing team. They kept playing so hard, even though it seemed like all the odds was against them. They seemed to never lose hope. They just kept pushing through.

It reminds me of the verse that reads, "I have seen something else under the sun: The race is not to the swift or the battle to the strong, nor does food come to the wise or wealth to the brilliant or favor to the learned; but time and chance happen to them all" (Ecclesiastics 9:11).

Sometimes situations occur in life where it looks like we have lost. It looks like the odds are stacked so high against us, that winning isn't even an option. We might as well throw in the towel and give up. However, God instructs us in His word that the race is not given to the person who is necessarily the best. The winner is not always the person everyone thinks will win, it's the one who endures to the end. It goes to those who keep their tenacity and don't give up. It's the one who knows that nothing is over until God says it's over.

With only four minutes left in the last quarter, the team that was losing the entire game stepped into the lead. They eventually won the game. Not only did they win the game but it was one of the largest comebacks to date in professional football. It speaks to the fact that, just because you feel like you have been losing your whole life, doesn't mean that God can't make you win at the end. You might come from a broken home, you might have been abused, you might have had a broken marriage, you might be a college drop-out, you might be going through all types of crazy bad breaks, and just wondering, "God when will I win?" Just know, when God is for you, who can be against you? As long as you stay with God you will always win if you don't give up. Keep moving forward. Your win is right in front of you. It might be hard, it might take a lot of endurance, but if you don't faint you will rise to the top.

WEEK 13

God Can Stop The Sun

"On the day the Lord gave the Amorites over to Israel, Joshua said to the Lord in the presence of Israel: "Sun, stand still over Gibeon, and you, moon, over the Valley of Aijalon." So the sun stood still, and the moon stopped, till the nation avenged itself on its enemies, as it is written in the Book of Jashar. The sun stopped in the middle of the sky and delayed going down about a full day. God had promised the Israelites that they would have the land that their enemies had occupied. The day that the Lord had given the Israelites the land of the Amorites, Joshua prayed a valiant prayer."

Joshua 10:12-13

Joshua asked God to hold the sun. Joshua asked him to basically make the earth stand still until they had finished fighting their fight.

I remember a girl I knew who was extremely behind in her studies. She was also tired, and the constant battle with her grades was sending her into fatigue. She asked the Lord to redeem her time so that she would be able to catch up with her classes. Sure enough, the worst blizzard the Northeast has seen in years allowed her an unexpected 3 days off from classes. In these three days, she was able to catch up on all the work that she had been lagging behind in.

God is still in the business of the impossible. Maybe you are facing a difficult problem in which the solution is so radical that you're too scared to pray for it. However, God said in His word, "Be strong, and of great courage, do not fear or be dismayed, for the Lord, Your God is with you wherever you go." Joshua 1:9

God will make the impossible happen! Don't be scared! When God was telling Joshua all the things that He would do for Him and Israel, He must have known Joshua was scared because He told Joshua several times to have faith and to not be afraid. God was with Him wherever he would place his feet.

God has promised you something. Maybe it's for success in business, maybe it's to get through med school. Maybe it's to get into school, maybe it's to get a new job, maybe it to have a baby, or get into a good relationship. God will make it so that you are having a surplus during a recession! God will stop things for you to get you where He has promised you to go. Yes, it might be scary, you might even be terrified, but keep pushing toward the mark of the prize of His High Calling in Christ Jesus!

You might not need God to hold the sun, you might need Him to hold a deadline, or to give you favor in a place you know you don't deserve to be. However, be encouraged because with God the things you don't deserve are the things that end up in the palm of your hands!

Your sun might be a bill that can't be paid or a deadline that has passed. Whatever your sun is, God can hold it so that you can get to your blessing!

WEEK 14

Follow The GPS: God's Positioning System

"Your word is a lamp for my feet, a light on my path."

Psalms 119:105

One day I was with a friend visiting the city. It was time for me to go home, so he offered me a ride. As we were riding around he let me know that he did not know the section of town we were driving in. I asked, "Do you have a GPS?" He responded yes, to which I said, "Then you shouldn't have a problem."

As we were driving in the unfamiliar part of town, I noticed that his face looked a little troubled. At this point, I asked him if he was okay and if he knew where he was going. To this, he said, "I don't know where I am, but I'm just going to follow the GPS and it will lead me where I am supposed to go."

You might be at a spot where everything seems pretty dark. You have no idea where you are going and what the next step is going to be. However, God is telling you to trust in Him and He will direct all your paths. It's funny how we can trust in a GPS system with all our hearts, however, when it comes to trusting God we hesitate. Did God not make the man who made the GPS? God holds the map to your life. Everything might seem unfamiliar, but He tells you to go. You might not know where God is taken you, but you will reach the destination if you keep following his directions.

Your GPS in life is God's Positioning System. God will tell you where to go, to get you where you need to be!

WEEK 15

Beware Of The Popcorn Machines

"The righteous person may have many troubles, but the Lord delivers him from them all."

Psalm 34:19

Working at a pharmacy always allows you to see children at work. Mothers with children in hand, step through the pharmacy doors while being amid errands. Paying attention to little children can help in our understanding of how God relates to us.

One day while being at the pharmacy, I encountered a woman and her child. At first, the child stood by his mother, being content and playing with the toy that he had. All of a sudden, something caught the child's eyes and he slowly wandered away from his mother. Eventually, the child was all the way by the popcorn machine, which is fascinating to look at because it is illuminated, but hot to the touch. As the child began to reach out his hand, the mother screamed his name to beckon him to come back.

The child looked at his mother and hesitated. He just wanted to touch the popcorn machine. As his mother saw the danger her child was in, she ran to him and grabbed him up and out of the situation he was in. At that point, the child started to cry saying, "Mommy you're ruining my fun!"

God is our deliverer, whether we want to admit it or not. Has there been a situation in your life, where you think God is totally raining on your parade? How come I can't get that job, or the awesome car, or the beautiful mate? How come I can't have what lights up my eyes?

We must learn that He does not think like us. We see something for the illumination, the light that it seems to omit. We just want to touch the popcorn machine. However, God sees that it's hot. The thing that we want might be so dangerous that it can hurt us. He will warn us to back away, but God will come and deliver his children eventually to keep them from hurting themselves past the point of return.

Therefore, God shuts doors. Sometimes God shuts doors in order to deliver you from a problem you were about to walk into.

For example, one day I was looking at an elevator in one of the tallest building in Pittsburgh. God then revealed to me that, "Although that elevator looks like it can take you to the top of the building, pay attention to it closer." I then looked and noticed that inside the elevator, there was no light. If I had stepped into it, I would have been completely in the dark and I would've gone nowhere. God is that voice that helps you when you are about to walk into a dangerous situation that you feel may elevate you, but will really put you in danger.

Back to the little boy and his mother. I thought of times in my life that God told me to get away from the popcorn machine, and I just had to touch it, burned myself, and ended up running right back to Jesus. I have seen children in the pharmacy do just that. They wander off, but when they come back hurt because they strayed away, their mothers always patch up whatever wounds they come back with.

That's how God is with us. He tries to tell us when things are going to hurt us and beckons us to come back. Even the pain that you endure now, might be because God was trying to keep you from a greater pain. The pain of losing a job, a friend, and relationship, might be because God was trying to keep you from a much greater pain.

We should always be encouraged that no matter what problems we face, God will always deliver us from all of them. He is our very present help.

The funny thing about us is that we see something and we think it is so great. I'm sure the little boy was convinced that touching the popcorn machine was going to change his life. However, he didn't know that I had candy waiting from him, as we give all the children coming to the pharmacy candy. When the child finally came back, his mother said he would not be getting candy until later because of his disobedience.

How many times have you forgone your own blessing because you don't want to listen to God when He was trying to deliver you from potential great pain? How many times will you ignore him, and miss out on an actual treat just to touch a popcorn popper?

Lord, help us to let go when you tell us to let go. Lord deliver us from the problems that we have put ourselves in by being stubborn. Lord help us stay close to you. We don't want to miss our blessing because of disobedience. Lord, strengthen us. God forgive us from straying away if we have. Amen!

WEEK 16

Why Are You Laughing?

Then one of them said, "I will surely return to you about this time next year, and Sarah your wife will have a son." Now Sarah was listening at the entrance to the tent, which was behind him. Abraham and Sarah were already very old, and Sarah was past the age of childbearing. So Sarah laughed to herself as she thought, "After I am worn out and my lord is old, will I now have this pleasure?" Then the Lord said to Abraham, "Why did Sarah laugh and say, 'Will I really have a child, now that I am old?' Is anything too hard for the Lord? I will return to you at the appointed time next year, and Sarah will have a son." Sarah was afraid, so she lied and said, "I did not laugh." But he said, "Yes, you did laugh."

Genesis 18:10-15

In this story, we see Sarah, an old woman who could no longer bear children. Sarah herself had heard a word from the Lord, and instead of receiving it, she laughed at it. When God asked why she had laughed, she even went as far as denying the fact that she did, since Sarah didn't laugh out loud. The text said she laughed inside of herself, so the only person who heard was the Lord.

How many situations have you not taken before God because you thought of them as too impossible for them to happen? How many times have you just not prayed? How many times has somebody declared a promotion, a new relationship, a new job, a new car, a new BLESSING, over your life and you just LAUGHED, some of you out loud, saying that will never happen?

Some of you are trying to act like you never laughed at God, knowing that you have had moments where you were like, "God, please, that will never happen!" God will make it happen, and the funny thing about this verse is that Sarah still didn't believe God, and He still blessed her anyway. Just like that verse, Numbers 23:19, "God is not human, that he should lie, not a human being, that he should change his mind. Does he speak and then not act? Does he promise and not fulfill?" If God said he's going to do it, He's going to do it, because, "if we are faithless, he remains faithful, for he cannot disown himself." 2 Timothy 2:13

Believe in the Lord. Nothing is too hard for God. In the text, it said that Sarah was past the age for her to have babies. Maybe you feel you are past the age to get married, or past the age to go back to school, or past the age to make a career change. The devil is a liar! Don't laugh at God when He tells you He can do anything. Laugh at the devil when he tells you God can't!

Let me list out some lies that the devil may be telling you. Your GPA is not high enough to get you into graduate school. You are too old to get married. You are too uneducated to ever make anything out of yourself. The dream you set out for yourself is too lofty to ever attain. No one is ever going to want you with all of the issues your family has. You're worthless. You're untalented. God will never redeem the time that you have wasted.

Stop listening to all these lies. They are not true. Nothing is too hard for God. Just tell yourself that. God can change any situation because he specializes in impossibilities.

WEEK 17

Study Before The Test

"For wisdom will enter your heart, and knowledge will be pleasant to your soul. Discretion will protect you, and understanding will guard you."

Proverbs 2:10-11

This weekend I attended a church sermon in which the pastor said something very profound. She said that "the teacher is always silent during the test." I thought this statement was very interesting, and once I pondered on it for a moment, God revealed so much about Himself.

Remember when you were in elementary school? Your tests were very easy, and if you had problems, you could always ask the teacher for help and she would guide you or at least give you a hint in the right direction. In our Christian lives, God will always give us tests. Tests are not made because God hates you, but it is to enhance your understanding of the concept at hand so that you will be able to progress in those subjects and in others in the future.

As you progressed through school, the tests got harder and harder. Just like in our Christian walk, the tests that you go through will not be the same. They will get more difficult. You cannot be an 11th grade Christian and still expect God to give you a kindergarten level test. They will get more challenging. As you continue in education, teachers do not give much assistance during the test. Why? Because of the answers are in the book.

When you think about it like that, it does not make sense as we go through life, not to read the handbook of life, which is the Word of God. Would you go to a test without reading and studying the book to prepare yourself? Would you skip class habitually if you wanted to make an A and find favor with the Professor? That's how our relationship with God is. You must read and study His Word if you expect to pass the test of Life. The great thing about being in "God's Classroom" is that even if you get it wrong the first time, you always have a chance to pick up your book, study a little more, and try again. AND you can always ask God for help if you don't understand, and He will surely direct you.

Having knowledge of His Word is our preservation. I encourage everyone who reads this, to tap more into reading His Word every day and apply it to your daily life. In order to pass the tests of life, we've got to open the Book.

WEEK 18

Even A Warthog Can Kill A Lion

"When he had gone indoors, the blind men came to him, and he asked them, "Do you believe that I am able to do this?" "Yes, Lord," they replied. Then he touched their eyes and said, "According to your faith let it be done to you."

Matthew 9:28-29

I was watching a documentary, and they were having a special on warthogs. Warthogs, as you might know, are very small animals. However, they are very aggressive. They tend to go after things that others might deem to be unattainable, and this was no different from the warthog on this show. The warthog was standing face to face with a lion. The lion towered over the warthog and seemed to have an advantage in every way. However, all the sudden the warthog prepared himself, and rammed its sharp tusks into the lion's jugular and almost instantly, the lion died. I had just witnessed a warthog killing a lion. Crazy right?

Sometimes if you want God to bless you big, you are going to have to go after things that people deem to be unattainable. To get a lion-sized blessing, you must have a lion-sized faith. The thing about it is, with God, all things are possible. Even if all the odds are against you. The warthog was small, and if I asked you if a warthog and a lion got into a fight who you would think would win, I know most of you would not say the warthog. You know why the warthog killed the lion? Because of the warthog's size, it was perfectly positioned to hit the lion straight in its weak spot. So once again, the warthog's struggle or its weakness has become its strength.

In the verses above Jesus healed the blind, but first, he asked them an important question. Do you believe? God wants to know if you believe because He will bless you according to your faith.

Maybe you are going through some things right now that are hard. Maybe you are unqualified, and maybe you just cannot see how God can give you such a great blessing when it is only little old you. However, God has designed you the way you are and has put you through some things for a divine purpose. And this purpose will lead you to do mighty things, even things that are impossible. Because remember, what is impossible with a man is possible with God. With God, you can be a warthog and kill a lion. However, you've got to have faith to go after your lion-sized blessing!

I pray that God helps strengthen your faith. It might be hard now, but God always has a plan, trust Him. God, I thank you for blessing us already. Lord I thank you for the God you are and how you create us with special talents that will help us in fighting for the blessings that the devil tries so hard to steal from us. Lord bless us with perfect faith. In Jesus name, Amen!

WEEK 19

Stay Alert!

"Be alert and of sober mind. Your enemy the devil prowls around like a roaring lion looking for someone to devour."

1 Peter 5:8

I lived in Pittsburgh for a long time, and the transition from winter into spring always followed the same cycle. Basically, around March it will get warm, and on a consistent basis. So warm, that the trees began to bloom and grow back. However, like clockwork, one random snow storm will kill all the flowers that had grown. It happens almost every year!

This is kind of how the devil works in your life. Things start to go well. God is blessing you left and right, and as Christians, we can tend to get lax when this happens. We start reading our bible less, and we stop going to church as often. We no longer cry to God the way we used to anymore because everything is going right. However, when everything is going right, that is when you need to pray more fervently than you did before. Why? Because the devil didn't forget about you! He's just planning his next attack. However, even though the devil is clever, you got a resource that can help you withstand what he tries to do, and that's Jesus.

Basically, the devil will catch you off guard. Just like new flowers in bloom, he will bring an unforeseen snowstorm to destroy you. Therefore, God tells us in His word to stay alert! No matter what happens do not get lax in your spiritual life, lest the devil traps you. It gets hard to remember to pray sometimes especially when things are going right. But we have to be prepared to pray on the offense.

When a football team is getting ready to face an opponent, they study tapes of the way that the opposing team plays so that they can be prepared when they face them on the field. You are going up against an enemy, so you need to start to learn how the devil attacks you. Think about times in your life where you felt attacked and you will realize that the devil was attacking you in your same soft spot. It might be in your finances, it might be in your family, it might be in your mental, emotional, or physical health. The devil will pick a place to attack you. However, don't be fooled, because although you might have conquered him in one weak place, he is already planning to go after another.

How to defend yourselves against attacks? Pray, and pray all the time, without ceasing. Pray every step you take.

If you ask God, to help you to see and be vigilant of what the devil's plans are, you will not always be getting up from being attacked. You'll be better prepared to withstand the attacks when they come. I pray that God helps us all to be spiritually on guard.

WEEK 20

God Is Your Friend, Treat Him Like One

"What shall we say, then? Shall we go on sinning so that grace may increase?"

Romans 6:1

Would you continue to talk to someone if they continuously ignored you? Or let's say you were trying to help someone, by giving them good advice, and they got mad at you, would you continue to be there friend? Or better yet, let's say someone stood you up, told you that they were going to do something and did not, would you continue talking to them?

I sincerely thank God for His grace, because sometimes, this is how we treat our own Heavenly Father. We ignore Him consistently, He tries to help us, and we get mad at Him. We will stop praying, or going to church, to see other people and do other things that will merit us nothing without Him. He gets us out of situations, and we put ourselves right back in the same mess and ask for His help, sometimes without even thanking Him for all He did.

When Paul speaks in Romans about God's grace, it really hit me. We often take it for granted and do our own thing when we want to. Only when things fall apart, do we humbly come back to Him to fix the problem.

Don't do things to God that you wouldn't like done to you. I know it sounds crazy, but think about it. Don't ignore God if you don't like being ignored. Don't stand God up if you don't like to be stood up. Trust me, if we can treat God the way we like to be treated, our relationship with Him will surely become better, and stronger. Start treating God like the friend He is to you. Not like someone that you call when you need something.

Today have a personal conversation with God. Just about what is going on, what you might need to happen, and just give Him thanks. Develop a real relationship with Him today. Just because you are a Christian doesn't mean that you have a perfect understanding of God. Learn more about Him, and I'm sure you'll be blessed.

WEEK 21

Killing Them With Kindness

"For it is God's will that by doing good you should silence the ignorant talk of foolish people."

1 Peter 2:15

There are so many things that one can realize from this verse. The first is that despite what people say about you, you should do good towards them. Why? Because doing good towards them as a service to God gives Him glory. Some people might say, "I am not about to let someone run all over me." However, doing good for someone who might be doing wrong towards you does not at all mean you are letting them walk all over you.

By no means do I mean you should stay in a bad relationship because when people do you wrong, correction is needed. However, I am saying that after you correct them in love, you shouldn't go out of your way to do bad things towards them. In this situation, you should ask God for direction. You should not wish horrible things to happen to those who do you wrong. One must know that nothing that a man could do to a person is worse than the vengeance of God. Hand people who have wronged you over to Him, and continue to bless people as your duty to the Lord, not as your duty towards them. When you do this you will realize that you won't feel used because you won't be doing anything for the person, but it will all be for God. Make sense?

But the second thing this verse says is that God wants you to do good to people so that they would have no room to say stupid things about you. Have you ever heard of killing people with kindness? Sometimes when you are nice to people who are mean to you, it stops them from saying anything bad about you. In a way, it can make the person feel worse than if you had given them back the same horrible attitude that they gave you.

Have you ever stopped to think if God returned you with all the things that you did to Him what your life would be like? Take a second to think about it. Those times where you have literally slapped God in the face by doing things that even your closest friend does not know you have done. However, God still loves you. I know that some of you might have had a moment where you realized how good God is to you, despite your bad actions. Now I want you to think of how you felt when you concluded that God was good to you in spite of you being so bad to Him at times.

This week if you are going through a painful situation with someone who has hurt you, ask God to teach you how to forgive them, and be kind even in the face of adversity. God, give us the strength to be nice, even when we don't feel like it. Help us to realize that we do it for You and not for the other person, Amen!

WEEK 22

No Fear In Love

"There is no fear in love. But perfect love drives out fear, because fear has to do with punishment. The one who fears is not made perfect in love."

1 John 4:18

Have you ever been scared to love someone? Have you ever been afraid to fall that hard for a person? I've noticed that today, love is mentioned along with the words pain, sorrow, and fear. We often hear the phrases pain is love. Or "love kills slowly," or even singers saying there is fear in love. I had to ask the question what exactly is love?

Well the Bible defines love in Corinthians as "Love is patient, love is kind. It does not envy, it does not boast, it is not proud. It does not dishonor others, it is not self-seeking, it is not easily angered, it keeps no record of wrongs. Love does not delight in evil but rejoices with the truth. It always protects, always trusts, always hopes, always perseveres." -- 1 Corinthians 13:4-7

Love has no fear. Love is not painful. Love is perfect. Why? Because God is love. God has these attributes. He is every single aspect in the verse of Corinthians. Therefore, if someone does not truly know who God is, they cannot truly know what love is. Yes, you can get close, however, to experience perfect love, you must have intimacy with a perfect God. Understand that love in its raw form is perfect, it is people who are imperfect and sometimes fail when it comes to the constructs of what love represents.

The word love is a serious word and it is not to be used loosely if you don't mean it. Since God=Love, saying you love someone and not meaning it, is almost like using God's name in vain. I tell people that love is not a feeling or an emotion, it's a choice. You choose to love a person. It involves several actions. It's not just how you feel, it's really what you do.

No one could ever love us the way God loves us. He is the essence of it! That's why He is so good at it. Remember that loves takes time, and love is a choice that one makes to stick by a person no matter what. Love people freely, but also know the implications. Love is a choice to be kind, to forgive wrongs, to be longsuffering, and not to be rude. You must be prepared if you want to make that choice when it comes to loving another person.

However, there is something in all of this we can take away. There is no fear in loving God, because the more we love Him, the better everything will seem to be. The more you love God, the more everything will start to fall in place, even if it's chaotic. God gives the peace that surpasses all men's understanding, and abiding in Him gives joy.

This devotional is for those who have been wronged and have become afraid to love. I pray that God helps you to learn how to love properly again. I pray that God helps you understand fully what love is so that when you see it in the counterfeit form, you would know and be careful. God will show you what love is, when He reveals Himself to you. Amen!

WEEK 23

Testing Before Release

"Not only so, but we also glory in our sufferings, because we know that suffering produces perseverance; perseverance, character; and character, hope. And hope does not put us to shame, because God's love has been poured out into our hearts through the Holy Spirit, who has been given to us."

Romans 5: 3-5

Most phones before they go out into the market have to go through test. In looking at different phones, I saw that they typically go through five rigorous tests before it is put on the market, these include the Tumble Test, Drop Test, Compression Test, Bend Test, and the Button Test.

Literally, the phone is tossed around, dropped, agitated, and pushed to the limit, on purpose, before it is released into the market. If the phone fails any of these tests, it is examined, and reconstructed so that it can better perform. Phone manufacturers do this so that when the phone is given to its end user, it can resist the normal wear and tear that phone's experience during the duration of their lifecycle.

Yes, God tests you. Why? It is because before He puts you on the market for anything, meaning a husband, a wife, and job, a new location, your purpose—he needs to know that you are going to be able to withstand the pushes and pulls that a new season is going to bring you to. Some of us are so ready to get to the next phase that we want to skip the testing process. Nobody likes getting tested. However, would you use anything that has not been tested? Would you pay almost $600.00 for a new phone, if you knew that they just created it and put it out there without running any test on it? No! What some of these phones go through before they are approved is a very painful process to watch. They are literally pushed almost to the limit of destruction so that if they do break under pressure, the creative geniuses behind the phone can fix the phone, and make it stronger.

That is the great thing about God. He will never push you to the point of destruction. He will never give you more that you can handle. Even though it seems like it, God knows your limit.

God wants to make you strong enough to have what it takes to reach your purpose. Just like the first verse says, suffering produces perseverance. The more you suffer, and the more trials you go through, the easier it is for you to get through them and come out shining. He also says in this verse that perseverance produces character. When you go through different scenarios and trials in your life, it will make you a different person, and it will help you realize that although God puts you through the fire, there is always hope because God loves you.

Even though you are going through it right now, know this, God is trying to make sure you are ready for the "end user". Meaning God wants to make sure you are settled enough inside yourself before he gives you a husband or a wife. God wants to make sure that you have complete faith in Him before He gives you the career of your dreams. God wants you to be content in the state that you are in before He moves you to that new location. God wants you to realize the value of money before He gives you loads of it. It's temporary. Just keep being strong, and know that God is with you, He wants the best for you, and He loves you.

WEEK 24

Dandelions

"You did not choose me, but I chose you and appointed you so that you might go and bear fruit—fruit that will last—and so that whatever you ask in my name the Father will give you."

John 15:16

It hurts to feel like you are being rejected. Whether it be a relationship, an opportunity, or even a friend rejecting you, it can hurt so much. Just that feeling of not being the "chosen one" can hurt us sometimes. We ask ourselves in relationships, "Why didn't he/she pick me to date," or "Why couldn't they pick me to go to that school," or "Why didn't that job hire me," because, in our eyes, we perfectly fit the position. However, when we do not get chosen, we feel rejected, and slightly worthless.

However, the first thing every believer should know is that God chose you before you chose Him. Why? Because he saw worth in you! Even if it seems no one in this world wants you, God wants you. However, in the verse above there is a qualification of the ones that God has chosen. He has chosen you so that you can bear fruit. God is the master farmer. We are in His garden. Now the great thing about God is He will pull weeds from around you so that you can grow and bear fruit. The problem with us is, we keep the weeds around us because in our eyes they might not seem like they are choking the life out of us.

Here's a story, my grandmother was very good at farming. I mean she could grow just about anything. When I was younger, I remember watching her in her garden. When I was a child I used to love dandelions. They were so bright and pretty to me. However, as my grandmother was tending to her garden she continuously pulled what I thought were beautiful flowers right out of the ground! She saw the disdain on my face, and since she didn't speak English, she replied to me, "Chidi, dirty!" Which I knew meant it was garbage. That was when my father relayed the harsh news to me, that these flowers I admired were weeds.

What has God pulled away from you that you thought was a flower but would have sucked the life out of your fruit? He could have made a relationship end because it was not fruitful. What does fruitful mean? It means that this person is not adding anything to your life. He might have cut an opportunity off because it would not have been fruitful to you. And sometimes, it might hurt! Just like I was hurt when I saw my precious dandelion being pulled out of the ground with such annoyance. It was because my grandmother knew that if these dandelions stayed in her garden they would rob the plants of their ability to produce the best fruit they could produce. Also, understand sometimes that God pulls people and opportunities away because he knows that there is something better coming down the line. He knows that if the relationship, opportunity, or situation does not cease to exist that you will miss a better blessing.

God is trying to rid you of all these weeds so that you could be in His perfect will. That way, whatever you ask, will be what God wants for you. Because what you want, will align with what God wants for you. It's time to do some cleaning. I want you to think of all the people and things that are not adding anything to your life, and let God prune them from you so that you can reach your destiny. Amen!

WEEK 25

God's Antiseptic Spray

"Dear friends, do not be surprised at the fiery ordeal that has come on you to test you, as though something strange were happening to you. But rejoice inasmuch as you participate in the sufferings of Christ, so that you may be overjoyed when his glory is revealed."

1 Peter 4:12-13

My mother always told me that emotional pain is worse than any physical pain you can go through. The reason for this is that it not only affects the body, it affects the mind. Emotional pain can stifle your relationship with other people, and most importantly your relationship with God.

Emotional pain happens for many reasons. The feeling of being betrayed or lied to, the end of a relationship, the loss of a job, a friend, or just the normal ups and downs of life can send you through a tailspin of emotions. This type of emotional pain can cause you to become bitter, angry, and lose faith in the people that love you.

Think of when you were young, and you would hurt your knee. I remember when I would cut myself, I just wanted my mother to leave it alone. I didn't want her to put antiseptic on it because I knew it would burn. However, she would always tell me, if I don't take the hurt now, I would be in for an even greater hurt later if my cut were to get infected.

What is an antiseptic? Well, they're medicines that slow or stop the growth of germs and help prevent infections in minor cuts, scrapes, and burns. Notice the word 'minor'. The things that can potentially wreak havoc in your life are minor. They are guys that are not worth it. They are women who just don't have a clue. They are jobs that are not going anywhere. They are minor and they are not worth your time, and the biggest part of it is they are hurting you. No matter how minor they are, they can cause serious damage if not attended to.

Sometimes we just want God to leave it alone. We can be in painful relationships, dead end jobs, or just simply bad situations and we want to ignore it. We don't want God to dress the cut because we know that it's going to require antiseptic spray and it's going to hurt badly. How many times have you stayed in a relationship because you were afraid if you left, it was going to hurt badly or stayed in a job that wasn't it because if you left, you were afraid it was going to hurt? Or you stayed being a friend to somebody who disrespected you out of fear that if you were lonely, it was going to hurt badly? The devil is a liar! We thank God for loving us when we don't properly know how to love ourselves. God will rip you away from the bacteria in your life that can potentially hurt you. And it might not be gentle! When God takes you away from a dead-end relationship, job, or situation, it will hurt you badly, however, it is better for God to save you now, and for you to just take that antiseptic, than for your cut to get infected. You know what an infected cut can do to your body? Some cuts get so infected that amputation must occur, and that is a lot more painful. What I mean is that if you don't let go, and let God, it is going to be a lot more painful later in life. Just handle the antiseptic now, because antiseptic is a lot better than anesthesia if you catch my drift.

God is trying to rid you of the parasites you have allowed to be around you. Let him get rid of it. And like the verse, don't see it as something that is strange. You are too precious to God for Him to let you go around with an open wound acting like it is not there. God is trying to heal you, and deliver you out of a bad situation. Thank God for delivering you. God says to rejoice so that you can give Him glory when He reveals Himself. Meaning, that thing that you are holding on to will reveal why it would have messed you up and trust me, you will be thankful to God for delivering you from it.

Remember this, when God sprays the antiseptic on your wound, the pain will only last a second. I know it might hurt now, but that pain is temporary. Joy does come in the morning.

Lord, I pray that this speaks to people who are hurt and their hearts wherever they may be. I pray that the person that needs to hear this, hears it and that they are blessed. Lord help them understand that their pain is temporary, and that joy will come. Lord help us to trust you when you try to remove us from a bad situation. Amen.

WEEK 26

Slammed Doors

"Paul and his companions traveled throughout the region of Phrygia and Galatia, having been kept by the Holy Spirit from preaching the word in the province of Asia. When they came to the border of Mysia, they tried to enter Bithynia, but the Spirit of Jesus would not allow them to"

Acts 16: 6-7

I remember when I was in junior high school, I had a reading teacher. Now when she would get mad at us, she would leave the room and slam the door shut. I want you to know, that when God closes a door, He doesn't just close it, He slams it shut. Why does God slam it shut? Well, when someone slams a door shut, it immediately gets your attention. When we are about to walk into a horrible situation, sometimes we don't even realize how dangerous a situation we are in. This is why God has to pop us back into reality and slam the door closed so that we do not walk in.

A slammed door can hurt your feelings. Have you ever had someone slam a door in your face? It takes you by surprise at times, and you can't help but to be hurt. However, if that has ever happened to you, you know that there was something on the other side of the door that you didn't need to deal with, and the best thing is to walk away.

Sometimes we mistake God closing a door for the devil battling us. I see some people in relationships, who say, "I'm just trying to get him/her to Jesus." Did God tell you that He was going to use you to do that? If God did not explicitly tell you that, then you need to let go and let God, because God does not need your help. Yes, God does use people, but you need to ask God exactly what He wants you to do, and it might be to walk away. Just like Paul, the Holy Spirit took them away from certain places to preach the word. We don't know exactly why, however, God always knows why He keeps you away from things, even when you have His best interest in heart. What a friend we have in Jesus, because he has our best interest at heart always, no matter what.

You might have had doors slam in your face. You might have had opportunities or relationships that ceased to exist. However, be encouraged. At least you didn't enter into the situation. Yes, it hurts for doors to slam, especially when they seem so promising. However, God knows what's best for you, and for every slammed door, there is an open place where God is calling you.

I don't know what door just slammed in your face and you might not know why that door is being slammed shut. But God has a purpose, and God has a plan. It hurts, but know that whatever is on the other side of that door would've hurt you more! God's got your back. Just have faith and keep trusting in Him.

WEEK 27

Cracking Crab Legs

"Commit to the Lord whatever you do, and he will establish your plans."
Proverbs 16:3

After my sister's graduation, my family and I went to a restaurant to enjoy all you can eat crab legs. As the six of us sat there, we struggled to get the meat out of the little legs, and were growing frustrated, and gave up. My mother then said, "You should let your Daddy do it, he is the master at breaking crab legs." One of my sisters tried hard to do it herself, and remained frustrated, while I knew of my father's talent and positioned myself next to him so he could do all the cracking and I could do all the eating.

Three plates of crab later, my sisters were letting my dad crack crabs for them as well. And by the time the third plate came around, I had gotten a hang of it so that I could help people who weren't as good. There were two different shapes of the crab legs. There is the claw and there are the regular legs. Now what our father told us about the claws is that they are the most difficult to crack, and although the claw gives meat, the "arm" of the claw does not give a lot of meat despite the efforts you put into it.

Some of us think we got it all figured out. We think that in life we can, "Crack the Crabs" ourselves without any instruction from God. Meaning, we think that we can go through life's problems without consulting God for guidance. This is when we get caught up and we up end frustrated with nothing to show for it. We work so hard and diligently for something, and we get nothing out of it. How many times have you worked hard for a relationship to work and come out with nothing? How many times have you worked hard at your job, only to reap menial benefits for you hard labor? How long has your business not taken off, despite all you do? The devil is a liar! God did not intend for that to be the case, however, God must be at the beginning and the end of every plan you make in this life. Don't e xpect a plan to work if you don't have God involved.

Also, asking God to give us direction is one of the best things you can do for yourself. I didn't know how to break the crab legs, but my Daddy did. You don't know what to do in your life, even if you think you do, you do not. Therefore, you need to position yourself close to the one that does! Notice, when you position yourself close to the one who does know, your workload becomes very small. Why? Because God starts to fight your battles for you. In the restaurant, all I was doing was eating the crab meat. Sure, I had to actually get the crabs, meaning faith without works is dead. Don't think you can just sit around doing nothing and expect great changes. However, if you literally hand over whatever you've gathered to God, just like I handed my plate of crab legs to my father, you will reap the benefits. This I know, because for the first time in my life, I got full strictly off crabs. That's another point. When you hand it over to God, He blesses you more than you even expected off the thing that you gave to Him. This could be your career, your talent, your money or your relationships. When you hand it over to God, He will make it more successful.

The moral of the devotional is give it to Him. Maybe you have been struggling with what God wants you to do with life, but give it to Him first, meaning give the problem to Jesus, and he will make it clear for you.

WEEK 28

Focus On Your Destiny

"Let us not become weary in doing good, for at the proper time we will reap a harvest if we do not give up."

Galatians 6:9

You have accomplished something. Why? Because you are not in the same place you were before. However, when you start to make progress, and when the enemy sees that you are about to hit your destiny that is when he will attack. Now I don't know if the devil attacks you the same way he tends to attack me, however, over my life I have realized that the devil tends to attack me in steps.

1. He will attack the things around you. Meaning the material things. Your car will break down, you will lose your job, money will start getting incredibly low, etc.

2. He will attack your calling. This is the purpose that God has set in front of you. This could be making less that superior grades, not measuring up to standards in the job, being demoted or displaced, or even having your reputation smeared.

3. He will attack your relationships. Your family, your marriage. If he couldn't get to you with the first two points, he will start to attack the people around you. This is when best friends become worst enemies. When people step out of your life that you never thought would leave. When romantic interest walks away.

4. He will attack your health. Suddenly, sickness will arise, whether it be the flu or cancer, he is trying to take you out by any means necessary.

5. The last thing the devil will attack is your own mind. He will put thoughts in your mind that will stop you from progressing in the calling that God has ordained for you. This is the worst attack because you can start to speak death into your own life.

However, we have had the devil attack us before. Since we know how he is most likely going to attack, we can fight on the offensive, instead of fighting on the defense. We can pray against what we feel might be coming before it even has a chance of coming.

This devotional is to let you know, that even though you might not think it, you have reached a point in life that is worth commending. Well done, however, now is not the time to start to lose hope. Now is not the time to digress. Now is not the time to start to get weak in your prayer life. Now is the time to start praying harder and stronger, because the devil will attack you again, in all these points in your life! Don't get tired, don't faint, and don't give up. God has a prize for you.

Focus on your future, not your past. God has a great destiny for you, and you are making moves towards it. And even if you haven't been living right, today by reading this devotional you are making one small step in the right direction.

Lord forgive us if we lost sight of You. Lord help us to understand that you have ordained us for a great destiny, and for us to not grow weary in our own well-doing. Lord, I pray you give us encouragement. Lord meet us at our individual points of need. Amen.

WEEK 29

Never Been Unloved

"For I am convinced that neither death nor life, neither angels nor demons, neither the present nor the future, nor any powers, neither height nor depth, nor anything else in all creating, will be able to separate us from the love of God that is in Christ Jesus our Lord."

Romans 8:38-39

I woke up one morning, wondering what God wanted me to write in this devotional. I sat in silence trying to wait on God to say something to me about what to write. He said, "Tell them how much I love them." God loves us so much. I know it seems so simplistic, but when you consider the selfish world and people who only love themselves, it's awesome to think of how great the magnitude of His love is. He loves you despite what you do to Him. Even though sometimes you fall beneath his Grace. Even though you are constantly imperfect. He is so consistent and so unfailing in His love. God is so jealous for us that He wants us to live our lives in daily communion with Him. It is beautiful to know that someone loves you so much that He wants to spend that much time with you.

No one can love you the way God loves you. No man, no friend, no family member. God is the only person that you don't have to be scared to love. You don't have to fear that He will hurt you. Because He's not going to. It's amazing love. It's perfect love. It's God's love. Bask in it. God's love letter is just to tell you how much you mean to Him. Never forget how much He loves you. To think that God loves you enough to simply tell you how much He loves you is more than amazing. To think that he would pause organizing the universe just to remind you that you are loved, cherished, and cared for, is extraordinary.

Lord, I pray for those of us who feel a lack of love in their lives. Help them know, that no matter who left them, no matter who deserted them, or went astray, that you have always loved them with a perfect love that is unbreakable. That love, cannot be shaken even by our own errors. Lord surround them with your love and grace this week. Amen.

WEEK 30

Dead Ends

"For the Son of Man came to seek and to save the lost."

Luke 19:10

One day I was driving around my neighborhood with one of my friends. We were going around a lot of curvy roads, and suddenly I realized that I didn't know where I was going. I continued to drive not knowing I was on a street that I was completely unfamiliar with. The street that we drove on had very narrow driveways. I was afraid to turn into them, so I kept on driving until I realized that the road I had chosen had no outlet. This was the point where I was forced to turn around in the large dead end. However, because I was so lost, I was so thankful for that dead end. Rejoice when a dead end hits your life. I know that might sound silly, but when God puts dead ends in your life he makes decisions become very easy for you. Sometimes we wander off God's paths, and when we do, and we don't have any direction, every way could look like potentially the right way. Also, when we are not going the way God intended us to go, things become very difficult. I reference this to Jonah. When Jonah went to Tarshish, instead of going to where God wanted him to go, his ship got wrecked, he got thrown overboard and ended up in the belly of a whale. It was there when he had no other choice that he was able to get back on board with Jesus so that he could accomplish the mission God had set out for him.

This is why you have to be happy about dead ends. They give you an opportunity to turn around. Dead ends make it easy to leave something behind because if you continue traveling on that road, you know for a fact that it won't lead you anywhere.

There are a lot of people reading this that are in dead end relationships. With friends, with jobs, and with situations. God is telling you that this is your dead end, and it's time to turn around. I pray that God gives you direction to go the way He wants you to go.

Lord thank you for making it impossible for us to continue on certain paths. Lord give us the wisdom to listen to your direction when we are on the wrong road. Lord, thank you for your wisdom, and I pray that you show us mercy if we are in the wrong place right now. Help us make better decisions. Amen.

WEEK 31

The Space Of Your Destiny

"For my thoughts are not your thoughts, neither are your ways my ways," declares the LORD.

Isaiah 55:8

I remember when I was learning how to parallel park, and my father was giving me some tips to help me out. His exact words were, "Make sure in the beginning you do the right thing, because what you do in the beginning will determine whether you enter that spot."

This is how life is. What you do in the start of a journey can determine how you end. Your own mistakes can cause you to waste a lot of your own time. How many times have you done something, and realized that it was not the right decision, and have to start all over again? Remember, just like parallel parking, if you don't make it into the spot, you're going have to drive out, and start all over again.

But we thank God that we have a Father, who knows better. We thank God that we have a Father that sees the 'spot' we want to be in. He is the person in the rear view mirror who is telling us when to stop, go, and turn the wheel in order to ensure that we get into the spot perfectly. What is great about God is, even though it may take you a little bit to get into the space, He will make sure you get into it if you trust Him.

You've got to trust God because He sees better than you. Another example with parking, is when I was with a friend, and she couldn't manage to get into a spot. I offered to go outside and direct her into the spot. Although she thought from her line of sight that she could not make it into the spot, from my line of sight, she plenty of space to navigate herself inside of the parking spot.

How many times have you passed up an opportunity because you thought you couldn't get it? How many times have you not applied for a job because you thought it was impossible? How many times have you not prayed, or given up praying for a spouse because you thought the person for you was too good to exist? How many times have you talked yourself out of a business venture because people said you wouldn't make it? The devil is a liar! The point is with God directing you, you can make it, even when it seems like you can't. Even when it is a tight spot, God can tell you where to go and what to do in order to get you into the place of your destiny.

The "space of your destiny" will not be easy to get into! It will be tight, and most likely you will have to re-adjust yourself, meaning you will have to change the way you live and the bad habits you possess, in order to fit into that spot that God has saved for you.

But remember, some spots are not meant for your car. Some of us have been trying to fit our SUV destinies into a compact car spot, and God is telling you to keep on moving and find a spot that fits.

Also, God is not a pass or fail type of God. If you don't make it in the first time, TRY AGAIN. Don't give up on God, because He won't give up on you. Just keep on trying, and keep on giving everything to God, and He will make you a success!

Lord, I thank you for being the person that is watching our backs. Lord we will give everything to you, and trust that you are steering us in the right direction. Thank you so much! Amen.

WEEK 32

The Grass Isn't Always Greener

"Lot looked up and saw that the whole plain of the Jordan was well watered, like the garden of the LORD, like the land of Egypt, toward Zoar. (This was before the Lord destroyed Sodom and Gomorrah.) So Lot chose for himself the whole plain of the Jordan and set out toward the east. The two men parted company: Abram lived in the land of Canaan, while Lot lived among the cities of the plain and pitched his tents near Sodom. Now the men of Sodom were wicked and were sinning greatly against the LORD."

Genesis 13:10-13

In this age where people determine a person's worth by material possession or academic prestige, it is easy for us to begin to compare ourselves to standards for us to decipher our own value. Some of us compare ourselves to other people in order make ourselves feel better.

However, sometimes we can compare ourselves to people and find that we are not equal and that by the world's standards, they might have it "better" than us.

Here are some issues that might make one feel that the grass is greener on the other side:

1. Other people's jobs make more money than mine
2. Other people's clothes are more expensive than mine
3. Other people's careers are doing better than mine
4. Other people are getting married way before me
5. Other people's cars are better than mine
6. Other people's families are not as dysfunctional as mine
7. Other people seem to have spiritual gifts, where I might not be as strong
8. Other people's bodies look better than mine

The list can go on and on. We as humans can find a million reasons to believe the grass is greener on the other side. This is why I turn to the story of Lot and Abram. Basically, there were two plots of land, and Abram gave Lot first dibs on which side he wanted.

Now Lot chose the side that was more lush and had more streams of water running through it which was seemingly the better side, and he settled there.

What Lot didn't know was that he was settling near Sodom, a place God ended up destorying.

Why I bring out of this story is sometimes we get so caught up in the hype that we don't realize that God is blessing us in our current situation. We get so lost in what seems good, that we forget to ask God what is *good*. We think we have it made, but what we don't realize is just like Lot settling down in Sodom, we settle for what we think is good, but is not God's will for our lives. Yes, the new guy we are dating might have a fancy car, but does he have good character? Yes, the new job might help us make more money, but will it be at the cost of our sanity? This seems really nice from the outside, but sometimes when you look a little more deeply, you will realize that some things are not all that they are cracked up to be.

Furthermore, the things that God has given us, and when he chooses to give them to us, are all for a reason. We don't know if Abram felt tricked when he was given the other plot of land that obviously didn't seem that good. However, that ended up being his saving grace because Sodom was destroyed. This is why it is important for us to not covet another person's situation. Don't bother about other people who got married, yours will happen in due time. Don't covet other people landing great jobs, yours will happen in due time. Don't covet the things that another might have because there is a distinct reason why you do not have it. God always knows, and He wants to make everything good for you.

Dear Lord, Help us to only live for an audience of One. Lord Jesus, help us to see that we shouldn't compare ourselves to anyone, but be content in the state that we are in. Amen.

WEEK 33

God's Esteem

"I will praise You, for I am fearfully and wonderfully made; Marvelous are Your works, And that my soul knows very well."

Psalms 139: 14

Self-esteem is something that many people struggle with secretly. Some people don't even know that they struggle with a low self-esteem. Often, low self-esteem is attributed strictly to women, but there are just as many men who deal with poor self-conception as women. In fixing issues with self-esteem, the first step is admitting that it's an issue.

Some of the top symptoms of low self-esteem in men are:

1. The inability to make a decision
2. Enormous amounts of shame
3. The need to be perfect

4. Inability to handle criticism

5. Overly pessimistic or critical

6. Constant worry about the future.

Although symptoms of female low self-esteem are somewhat similar, some common factors are always focusing on the past instead of the present, putting oneself down and not recognizing one's achievements, or having a low level of self-awareness— putting a lot of effort in maintaining a false image.

My prayer is that those of us who have low self-esteem would recognize it now so that they too can move over this hurdle.

This is the main problem with self-esteem. People are constantly telling us that there are things that we should do in order to make us feel better about ourselves. It is SELF-esteem right? Wrong. Having a healthy self-esteem is having a good understanding of how your heavenly Father views you. Therefore, it is not self-esteem, but God's Esteem. In the verse in Psalms 139: 14, David says, "I will praise You, for I am fearfully and wonderfully made; Marvelous are Your works, And that my soul knows very well."

God didn't make any mistakes on you. That is why when you talk down on yourself, you call God a liar. You tell Him what He made is not beautiful or marvelous. Just as God created the world and it was good, God created you and you are good. This is the biggest lie that the devil continues to tell people, and this lie can keep you from reaching your destiny.

In the book of Matthew, the Bible says to love your neighbor as you love yourself. God did not intend for you to hate the person you see when you look into a mirror. God wants you to love yourself. Why? Because that is one of His commandments to us. Loving yourself is a part of following God's word. This does not mean being conceited or being proud. This all has to do with having a healthy self-image and seeing ourselves the way Our Heavenly Daddy sees us.

Lord, I thank you because you have made us in your image and we are fearfully and wonderfully made. Lord, I pray that you help whoever it is to know that they are beautiful, and they are a success. Help them not to believe what the devil has told them about themselves. Lord help them to see that they are more than conquerors in Christ Jesus. Amen!

WEEK 34

Walking Over Money

""What have you done?" asked Samuel. Saul replied, "When I saw that the men were scattering, and that you did not come at the set time, and that the Philistines were assembling at Mikmash, I thought, 'Now the Philistines will come down against me at Gilgal, and I have not sought the Lord's favor.' So I felt compelled to offer the burnt offering." "You have done a foolish thing," Samuel said. "You have not kept the command the Lord your God gave you; if you had, he would have established your kingdom over Israel for all time. But now your kingdom will not endure; the Lord has sought out a man after his own heart and appointed him ruler of his people, because you have not kept the Lord's command."

1 Samuel 13:11-14

Busyness can make us walk right over the blessings that God had for us. During work at the pharmacy where I worked at years ago, the days could be long. With hundreds of customers to attend to, sometimes it's easy to ignore the obvious. I had a ten-dollar bill tucked in my pocket. Since there were so many other things to pay attention to, I wasn't paying attention to all to my surroundings. There was so much to do! Scripts needed to be filed, a line was starting to form, and I was just so busy. As one of the customers waited in line, she noticed that the ten dollar bill that was in my pocket had landed on the floor because I was running around. The customer tried to get my attention, however, I was so busy with other things that I wasn't listening, and she did not have a loud voice. However, everyone in the pharmacy, including myself were too busy to notice. When she pointed it out she said, "I just thought it was odd because you guys were so busy that you literally kept walking over money."

Everyone is guilty of being distracted. Life happens and busyness occurs and before we know it we become so distracted by everything going on around us that we literally forget to hear God's voice. Saul had a commandment from God, however, Saul got distracted. If you look at the verse, it says, Saul saw the Philistines were about to attack, then he saw Samuel wasn't there when he expected, so then Saul, felt compelled to start doing things that God didn't tell him to do.

Stop listening to the noise, and try to hear God's voice before you get distracted with everything that wants to distract you. Because there will be noise, but the trick is, you must be able to remain focused in order to hear God and move in the direction He wants you to move.

This is when Samuel tells him what he did wrong, and tells him basically if you would've listened to God and kept his commandments you would have established your kingdom. I was so distracted by everything else that I was stepping and walking over my own money or in this metaphor my blessing. God has given us all something, something special. However, if we are careless with what God gives us, we can end up forgoing what God intended for us.

If you saw someone walking over money, wouldn't you think it was ridiculous? That is what some of us do. We are so distracted that we don't see the blessing God gave us that is right under our nose. We don't see it because we are too busy attending to everything else.

How many times have you moved and not asked God what he thought before you did it? How many times have you felt compelled to do something, but at the end of the day you were not spiritually led? How many times have you dated someone and not asked God what he thought first? When you don't obey God, you end up forgoing blessing that He intended for you to have. The trick is, NEVER become so distracted that you cannot hear what God is trying to tell you. God's not going to shout out to you but he does talk to you. He is that still quiet voice. Just like the woman at the pharmacy, but if you are not still enough to hear it, you are just going to keep walking all over your blessing and not realize it.

We will not walk over the blessings that God has intended for us because of disobedience, and not listening to God. God will establish us, if we listen, trust, and obey. Amen!

WEEK 35

Tomatoes Seeds Harvest Tomatoes, Not Peppers

"Do not be deceived: God cannot be mocked. A man reaps what he sows. Whoever sows to please their flesh, from the flesh will reap destruction; whoever sows to please the Spirit, from the Spirit will reap eternal life. Let us not become weary in doing good, for at the proper time we will reap a harvest if we do not give up. Therefore, as we have opportunity, let us do good to all people, especially to those who belong to the family of believers."

Galatians 6:7-10

When I was in high-school I used to spend a lot of time in my father's backyard. He just came home and I went to greet him as he was watering a plant outside. My father then asked me what I thought the plant was. To me, it looked like a pepper. He then corrected me and told me it was a tomato. I asked, "Is it like a pepper tomato or something?" (Excuse my ignorance, but they really did look like peppers) And my father said, "No Chidi, you can't plant tomato seeds and expect peppers."

The scripture reading for this week talks about reaping what you sow. Now in my lingo, this is what I felt the verse read, "Don't trip, ain't nobody gonna try to play God. Because you get what you give."

Laugh if you want to, but honestly, it's in our best interest to remember that God is never made a fool of. Laziness does not reap promotion. A deceitful man will not stay with a good woman. A manipulative woman will not stay with a good man. It doesn't add up. You can't act completely ridiculous and expect great results because that is not going to happen. You can't plant pepper seeds and expect tomatoes.

Whatever it is you put into something is the same you will get out of it. You spend time with God and handle God's business, guess what? God will handle your business and your situations. If you are nice to others, people will be nice to you. If you treat people badly, people will treat you badly. If you're always closed to others, people will not open up to you. That's just how it works, simple and plain.

And I'm not saying that God does not grant favors. There are some things that you did not necessarily deserve that you received. However, as Christians, we need to know that God cannot be fooled. You cannot continue living one way and expect the results to be completely the opposite of the way you have been living. Don't get me wrong, good deeds don't get you into heaven, however doing good towards others and God will make you live a more abundant life. It's God's commandment to love God and to love people. To love our neighbors as ourselves. In Luke 6:38 it reads, "Give, and it will be given to you. A good measure, pressed down, shaken together and running over, will be poured into your lap. For with the measure you use, it will be measured to you." Do right towards God and towards others and watch your life change.

This week I charge everyone, to make an extra effort to love God and to love the people around us. Do to others as you would want to be done to you. Amen!

WEEK 36

What Did God Say?

"Then the word of the Lord came to Jonah a second time: "Go to the great city of Nineveh and proclaim to it the message I give you." Jonah obeyed the word of the Lord and went to Nineveh. Now Nineveh was a very large city; it took three days to go through it. Jonah began by going a day's journey into the city, proclaiming, "Forty more days and Nineveh will be overthrown." The Ninevites believed God. A fast was proclaimed, and all of them, from the greatest to the least, put on sackcloth."

Jonah 3: 1-5

It is important to know what God wants you to do and to follow Him when He says to do it. Why is because you make life a lot harder for yourself when you are not walking in His path. What seems better can sometimes not be what God planned for you. I turn to the story of Jonah because Jonah is not a lot different from most of us. Here we have a man who was blatantly told by God to go somewhere and deliver a message. However, he did the stark opposite because of what he thought, and partially because of his own fear.

The first lesson we learn is you can't run away from the calling God has for your life. You can prolong it, but you cannot run away. Why? Because God will pursue you until you do what He wants you to do. God pursued Jonah and didn't give Him rest until Jonah finally agreed to do what God wanted him to do. Here's a way to know when you are not in the will of God, when despite everything you do you keep ending up right back at the place where you left God's calling and started doing your own thing.

The reason why I picked this verse is because when Jonah finally started to follow what God wanted him to do, God helped him on his journey. Notice, the journey was supposed to be three days long, however, Jonah made it into the city within a day. When you do what God wants you to do, God can redeem your time. When you do what God wants you to do, yes it might be hard, but God can make it easier than you thought it would be, or easier than it is for most people. When you do God's business, God will handle your business.

That is why it's important to be in God's plan not your plan. God's plan is not always the most attractive. It's not always the one that seems like it makes the most money. It's not always the one that will make you an immediate success. It's not always the one that a lot of people will agree with but please believe me when I say, that God's plan is always better than yours. Listen to what God is telling you, not what you are telling yourself. Surely God will direct your paths to success, despite what it is.

WEEK 37

A Bitter Pill To Swallow

"Not only so, but we also glory in our sufferings, because we know that suffering produces perseverance; perseverance, character; and character, hope."

Romans 5:3-4

Suffering from a cold is the worst. Between the sore throat, coughing, and sneezing, you could just want to crawl into a ball and cry. Once I had a sore throat so severe, that I couldn't sleep. Not to mention all the other symptoms of your typical cold. That night, I thought to myself, I am going to get some cough syrup to coat my throat. Went off to the store and I got it, only for it not to work and it kept me up ALL NIGHT. When 6 am rolled around, I was tired, cranky, and my throat was on fire. Now there is a medication my mother used to give me when I was little. I hated it, but it always worked. The taste made me nauseous, but all I could think about was relief. After not sleeping and being in pain, I was desperate! I bought a pack of the medicine I hate, and what do you know, some relief, after a night of pain.

As I sipped on the medicine, I thought of how you feel when you go through tough times you just want it to end. You just want God to take the pain away. Sometimes you run to the one thing that will not help you. We run to friends, we run to family members and we still end up in the same "sick" disposition that we were in the first place.

Also, sometimes God puts you through something in order to make you better. Have you ever been in a situation in which after you came out of it, you had more patience, you were more resilient, or your faith increased? However, do you remember how low of a place you were when God was trying to teach you these things? Sometimes you are emotionally sick, however, the medicine (faith, patience, etc.) is a hard pill to swallow. The medicine for people doing you wrong is forgiveness, the medicine for someone cursing you is to bless them, but the remedy is not always easy to digest.

Often times when we are emotionally sick, we are also spiritually deprived. However, the last thing we want to do is take that nasty medicine. The last thing we want to do is go to Jesus. We want vengeance, we want to cuss the person out, and we want to make them feel as bad as they are making us feel. We don't want to take the nasty medicine of doing the right thing and walking on the straight and narrow path. Why? Because being nice when someone is nasty to you is a bitter pill to swallow. But in the end, it will make you better.

God is telling you to take the medicine of His Word. Take the vitamins of Jesus to make you strong. What is His medicine? It's praying about the things that bother you. It's reading your Bible and allowing the words to soak in your spirit and reflect in your actions. It's taking the high road, even when it's the hardest. Yes, it hurts. He knows it hurts. It hurts when that relationship failed. It hurts when you lost that job. It hurts when your friend betrayed you. It hurts when people in the church wouldn't accept you. It hurts! However, take God's medicine. It might not taste good at first. It might hurt to swallow it. It might be difficult, but I promise it will make you feel better. Know that in your suffering, God is doing a new thing. In the pain of swallowing the medicine, know that if you give it time, the medicine will work to heal your body.

WEEK 38

It's Not About You!

"And so it was with me, brothers and sisters. When I came to you, I did not come with eloquence or human wisdom as I proclaimed to you the testimony about God. For I resolved to know nothing while I was with you except Jesus Christ and him crucified. I came to you in weakness with great fear and trembling. My message and my preaching were not with wise and persuasive words, but with a demonstration of the Spirit's power, so that your faith might not rest on human wisdom, but on God's power."

1 Corinthians 2: 1-5

People will make you think that the only way you will get to where you need to be is your intellect. The only way that you will get that job is if you go to the a certain school, the only way you will get into a relationship is by having a certain type of clout, or the only way you will ever have success is if you rake in degrees and accolades.

Again, the devil is a liar.

So many times I have heard people boast about how the degree that they obtained will get them what they desire in life. What they do not understand is you can think that you have it all together. You can have a perfect GPA, perfect personality, a perfect bankroll and end up nothing without God.

Just like John 15:5 says, "I am the vine, you are the branches. He who abides in me and I in him, bears much fruit; for without me, you are nothing."

Do not walk about this life thinking that you are the reason for your accolades. Do not walk around thinking that these things make you any better than anyone else.

Just like Paul said to the church at Corinth, he didn't come to them knowing any fancy words or rhetoric, but he just came with the knowledge of Christ, and that was sufficient. Paul knew that on his best day, it would never compare to God.

My brother always used to say this phrase, "It's not about you!" The sooner you realize that you are nothing without God, the more you will understand that success is not at all in your hands.

Maybe you want to do something unconventional. You don't want to go the safe route and you feel opposition from people. Maybe you want to be a writer, or a musician, or a hair stylist, and you feel people just don't understand and discourage you. Hold on to that because in Proverbs 18:16 it says, "A man's gift makes room for him and brings him in the presence of great men."

Encourage yourself, tell yourself that, my God given talent will make room for me and bring me in the presence of great people!

Maybe you are going through a situation where the odds are all against you. You feel like you are not smart enough to do the things that you desire to do. Don't let the things of this world define who you are. God is in control! You might not be able, but just like Philippians 4:13 says, "You can do ALL things through Christ!" Be encouraged! You can do anything with God.

Remember God is in the business of impossibility!

Lord help us to understand that it is not by might, or power, but by You that things are accomplished in our lives. Lord help us to rely on you. Not on our own intellect, but on your divine wisdom. Help us not to ask why, but to just trust.

WEEK 39

Favor Ain't Fair

"Josiah was eight years old when he became king, and he reigned in Jerusalem thirty-one years. His mother's name was Jedidah daughter of Adaiah; she was from Bozkath. He did what was right in the eyes of the Lord and followed completely the ways of his father David, not turning aside to the right or to the left."

2 Kings 22: 1-2

Favor is not fair. The first thing we have to realize is the blessings that God bestows upon us, are not because we are so qualified to get them. When God puts you in a position, it does not mean that you are qualified. It does not mean that you deserve it. Actually, it might be the latter, that you don't deserve it, and that you are unqualified. However, it does not mean, that God will not give you the ability to be in the high position that He has placed you.

One of the devil's tricks is he tries to cloud your mind with qualifications. He tells you; don't apply for that job, you're unqualified. Nobody is ever going to marry you, you know what you've done in the past, you're not fit to be a wife. Don't even talk to that woman, you don't have enough money! You're not good enough. Don't even think about applying to school, because you can't get in.

Josiah by the world's standard was not qualified. He was eight years old. He was a baby! God chose Josiah to rule the country. It didn't matter whether he deserved it or not. And it was not because of Josiah's ability that he could rule, it was because he kept focused on God and he didn't sway to the right or the left, and through God, he could do the job God placed him to do. You don't have to be qualified to be called to a purpose.

Maybe you are dealing with something. You don't think you are qualified, and you don't believe that God can do it for you because of your own shortcomings. God is telling you to try anyway! See how the Lord blesses you. God will put you in places that you didn't even think were attainable if you just trust in Him. Don't look around to your friends, because they will tell you not to try. Don't look to your family, because they too, might even disappoint you. If you are believing God for something, take your eyes off of yourself and your own shortcomings and look up to an Almighty God!

WEEK 40

Don't Miss The Point

"Blessed are those who find wisdom, those who gain understanding, for she is more profitable than silver and yields better returns than gold."
Proverbs 3:13-14

A lot of times I have been asked the question, "What is the difference between being smart and being wise?" My answer is being smart has to do with knowing facts. It has to do with being quick on your feet, and clever in different ways. However, wisdom has more to do with application. It is the knowledge gained from experience, and the understanding obtained from perseverance.

You don't need to open a book to be wise. You don't have to have a degree or be a scholar. True wisdom comes from God, and only from Him. This is why you shouldn't despise the hardships God puts you through because through experience you become a wiser human being.

Only through experiences can you truly become wise, whether it is the experience of watching another person or the experiences that you have gone through yourself.

As we go through trials, the experiences we go through make us wiser and stronger. My prayer for all of us is that we can understand key takeaways when God is trying to teach us lessons. For example, have you ever listened to someone teach about something, and after a long talk about numerous things, tells you to take away a couple of important points from the lesson? That is what I feel like God does. He puts us through a lot of things for us to take away the key lessons.

Our job is to make sure we don't miss the main point. Understand that in life you are given a test. If you fail the test, you must be examined again in that area. This week, take some time to look at your successes and your failures. Try to understand what God is trying to teach you from the things that have happened to you and make sure you are getting the key takeaways so that the next time a similar difficulty comes, you pass the test with flying colors. In addition, always remember that failure is only true failure when you fail and do not learn. Failure is only a lesson to your next victory.

WEEK 41

A Light In Darkness

"For his anger lasts only a moment, but his favor lasts a lifetime; weeping may stay for the night, but rejoicing comes in the morning."

Psalms 30:5

There are times in our lives where everything seems dark. It starts to seem as if things haven't been going right, and won't start to go right. A loss of a loved one, a relationship, a job, or anything else we hold dear can send us into a tailspin of emotions. If we don't focus on God during these moments, it could lead one to feel depressed, broken-hearted, angry, and empty. There is something special about this verse that God reveals to us, which is the difference between darkness and light. Sadness endures only when life gets dark. When you live in darkness, life gets very confusing. The opposite of living in darkness is living in light—or living and abiding in God.

Here is a story to help. One rainy summer day, the electricity got cut off in my apartment. Not only did I come in drenched from the rain, but I was extremely hungry, and to walk into a dark house was very saddening. I sat there for hours in the dark. Although I had candles, they still did not give the type of light needed to function in the midst of the night. Not only that but it began to get extremely hot and uncomfortable. When I finally surrendered to the fact that the situation was not going to change anytime soon, I did the only thing I could do at the time. Sleep, rest, and wait until the morning. Finally, I woke up and I was in a fully illuminated house. It was such a relief to feel the cool breeze of air-conditioning, and the taste of a warm cooked meal.

When life gets dark, you may feel like you are disconnected from God. You may feel empty, however, this may be a time that God wants you to be still and wait for Him to move. The hope in the verse is that "Joy comes in the morning". The verse is very metaphorical. God is the "morning" so even if it is dark as long as you live your life in the morning, i.e. God, you will have joy!

It is all about focusing on Him. Even when life gets dark, focus on the Lord and He will be your Light in the midst of the darkness. He will be your strength when you want to give up. He will be the love you need when you feel alone. Most of all God is your comfort. He is the Light in the midst of all the darkness that surrounds you. Focus on him, and you will not fall, and you will not stumble. It might be very hard to focus on him, especially when there are so many distractions. Especially when you hit points in your life that you don't have a solution. Just like sleeping in the midst of a blackout, you must rest in Him when you don't know what to do, and wait until he gives you a signal to do something.

Be encouraged. God knows everything you are going through. He understands. In Psalms 34:17-19 it says, "The righteous cry out, and the Lord hears them; he delivers them from all their troubles. The Lord is close to the brokenhearted and saves those who are crushed in spirit. The righteous person may have many troubles, but the Lord delivers him from them all."

God knows that you are hurting. He is your Comfort if you let Him in!

Amen!

WEEK 42

100% Returns

"Give, and it will be given to you. A good measure, pressed down, shaken together, and running over, will be poured into your lap. For with the measure you use, it will be measured to you."

Luke 6:38

I remember a story of a woman giving her tithe. She had just gotten a promotion on her job, and her tithe now was far more significant than it had been the previous month. Of course with the new influx of money, she could have bought a new pair of shoes, a bag, or even taken a vacation. There happened to be a special event at church in which the pastor had requested everyone to give as God led them, the first fruits of their increase. He encouraged them to give a little more than usual. The woman felt led to give, pulled $120.00 out of her wallet and gave. She was so thankful for what God had done for her, she felt it was the least she could do.

A couple days later, her new manager called her to the side. She wondered if she was in trouble. She dreaded walking to her desk. As she sat down, her manager let her know that she would be getting a bonus. The amount? $12,000.00. Literally, 100 times more than she had given.

There is one promise that God has for us. If you give, He will give back to you. If you give out of the goodness of your heart, God will bless your seed. It is similar to when you do not give. When you are stingy, you will always find yourself in want. However, when you give out of what God gives you, He will give you more. When God gives you a blessing, He wants to be sure that he can trust you with it. If I give you that new car, will you pick people up from church? If I give you more money, will you tithe? If I give you more time, will you spend it with Him? If I give you a talent, will you use it for my glory? If you do right with what God gives you, He will be sure to give you more. God is the best investment you can have.

If you invest in God, you can be sure that the fruits of your investment are joy unspeakable. The fruits of investing in God are a life of peace, happiness, stability, and blessing. This week, take some time to spend with God on your own. Really try to focus and listen to what he's saying to you. I pray for whatever you have spent with God, you will get a 100% return.

WEEK 43

Unconditional Love

"And have you completely forgotten this word of encouragement that addresses you as a father addresses his son? It says, "My son, do not make light of the Lord's discipline, and do not lose heart when he rebukes you, because the Lord disciplines the one he loves, and he chastens everyone he accepts as his son."

Hebrews 12:5-6

I remember one day my first nephew was playing around in my apartment. He was running about, as he normally does. I turned and saw that he somehow managed to grab a dime and ran full speed ahead toward the socket. As I saw what he was going for, I screamed out, "Don't you even think about it!" Right then he stopped dead in his tracks, dropped the dime, and began to bellow out in tears. After this, he stayed away from me, afraid that he was going to get into more trouble.

I remember when I was a little girl, and my mother used to yell at me for different child-like things I got into. I remember thinking "If mommy yells at me, she doesn't like me anymore." Or "Mommy is mad at me." Here I was looking at my nephew who was simply crying because he got in trouble and thought his Aunt was mad at him. Now he was avoiding me out of shame, guilt, and fear.

The truth is, I didn't yell out of anger. I yelled because I didn't want him to hurt himself. I yelled because I love him so much that I would never want any harm to come to him under my care. That is how God is with us. The Word says in Hebrews 12:6, "He chastises those whom He loves." God loves you, that's why he doesn't want you to hurt yourself. He will give you warnings in order to keep you from something that will cause you great pain if you mess around with it. Sometimes we may feel like God is punishing us, or like he is mad at us, however, the Word also tells us that God's anger is slow and it only lasts a second but his favor is everlasting! We don't need to be afraid of our heavenly Father. He looks out for our best and this is why sometimes He keeps us from things that we think are good for us.

Don't run away from God when you get into trouble! That is the worst thing you can do. Run to God. He is your refuge, and He is always waiting with open arms to accept you back! Don't let shame, guilt, or fear keep you from the presence of the Lord. As my nephew was avoiding me, I walked up to him and wiped his tears. I kissed him on the cheek and told him it was going to be okay, and why I yelled. I said, "I love you but I don't want you to hurt yourself." Even when we do wrong things, God still loves us. You can't do anything to separate you from that love. The Bible says in Romans 8:38, "For I am convinced that neither death nor life, neither angels nor demons, neither the present nor the future, nor any powers, neither height nor depth, nor anything else in all creation, will be able to separate us from the love of God that is in Christ Jesus our Lord." Nothing can separate you from His love. Absolutely nothing.

God's love is unconditional. There is nothing that can separate you from it, but sometimes God has to discipline us when we get on the wrong path. It is only for our best.

WEEK 44

Vengeance Is The Lord's

"Moses answered the people, "Do not be afraid. Stand firm and you will see the deliverance the Lord will bring you today. The Egyptians you see today you will never see again. The Lord will fight for you; you need only to be still." Then the Lord said to Moses, "Why are you crying out to me? Tell the Israelites to move on."

Exodus 14:13-15

It was hard for them. They had three mouths to feed, and both were working jobs that paid them pennies. Here they were, a young married couple from a distant place, trying to make it work. With no assistance from the government, because they were foreigners, they had to make ends meet by any means possible. As if it wasn't bad enough, soon the deportation committee was on their back. If something didn't happen quickly, they would be deported within a week. The man handling this couple's deportation hearings was mean and did not want to give them more time to get a visa. With no money for a lawyer, the couple asked a friend who was in law school to defend them. As they arrived in court, the deportation officer never showed up. What happened was the night before the hearing he died in his sleep of natural causes. Because he didn't show up to court, the case was thrown out.

And 30 years later, my parents, now American citizens live to tell about it.

We all go through unfortunate situations in our life where we are justified in wanting revenge. That guy broke up with us in cold blood, that friend stabbed us in the back and walks around like it's nothing, that job laid us off for no apparent reason. We all have things in our lives that we wish we could "take care" of ourselves. These things can leave us in a state of uneasiness and lack of inner peace.

In the verse above God is talking to the Israelites. They had been oppressed by the Egyptians for years, however, what were God's instructions to them? First, he says do not be afraid. Now in the text, the fear I believe that God was talking about was the fear that the Egyptians would capture them again after their freedom, the fear they would be killed. However, when we go through things sometimes we have a fear that if we don't do something about it, then nothing is going to get done.

God didn't tell us to handle these situations where we want revenge ourselves. We must remember vengeance does not belong to us. I don't care if you just want to tell someone off in the name of calling it correction. If even an inkling in your body gets some gratification because you let the person have it, that is where you overstep your boundaries. Don't get me wrong, correction is key, but not to make your adversary feel just as bad as you do. At the end of the day, you are accountable for everything you say and do. You are not justified for taking vengeance out on someone, and you can try to sugarcoat it all you want, but God knows your heart.

God said in the verse to be still. Sometimes in these situations God just wants us to stop moving. Stop trying to make sense of it. Stop trying to figure out whose fault it is. Just be still and let God handle it. His yoke is easy and His burden is light! There is no reason for you to go about life stressed over anybody! Let God fight your battles, and you will hold your peace, just as the verse says.

Someone reading this is really having a hard time dealing with revenge. This person did you wrong, and you are completely justified to feel how you feel. However, you are not justified to do what you are about to do. Think about it, because you are held accountable for your own sin whether the other party was right or wrong. Be encouraged. God sees the tears you cry. Don't ever think that God isn't doing something! God will come to your aid right in the nick of time. Just like my parents' situation, now do not get me wrong I am by no means saying that whoever is making you sad is going to hit the floor and drop dead tomorrow. However, I am saying that God will have his vengeance on the people who are hurting you. It's a promise. Doesn't mean you should go about wishing ill will on people, you just do what you are supposed to do for your enemies. You know what that is? Bless those who curse you. God never said pray hell fire on the people who do you wrong.

I really hope you are encouraged today to just keep believing that God is going to fight your fight. Amen!

WEEK 45

Sorting Stuff Out

"I will turn their mourning into gladness; I will give them comfort and joy instead of sorrow."

Jeremiah 31:13

No matter how long you try to put it off, you've got to eventually do laundry. If you're like me, you will wait until the bitter end for you to just take a day out and do all the laundry. While I was doing a large load that was taking forever to dry, I was a little upset. Why? Well, since I had waited so long to do the laundry I had already spent $10.00 worth of quarters and still had 2 loads that needed to be washed. However, it had to get done. As I was taking the large load out of the dryer, I found $5 rolled up in the dryer.

That made me think of when we go through valleys and wintery seasons in our lives. It is so hard to see the good part of a situation when it is so bad. God wants to tell you that even though you are in a messy situation, if you take it to God, He will clean up your situation, and something good will come out of it. Things in our lives are just like laundry. There are times when it's all good, new and clean, and there are times that things are dirty. We might have to even get rid of things in order to make room for new ones.

What I am trying to say is that if you don't do the 'laundry' in your life, you will never get a chance to experience how God is trying to bless you. If I would have never done the laundry, I would have never found the $5.00, and I wouldn't have as many options of clothes to wear.

The laundry in all of our lives are different. Some of us have to clean our lives of the relationships that we entertain. Some of us have to clean our lives of bad habits that we have allowed to form over the years. Some of us have to clean up the way we have been treating God and our prayer life. Nobody knows what's in your laundry basket except you! It's your responsibility to make time to clean up some of the messes in your life, however, God is always there to help you sort. He doesn't want you to wash your loneliness load with a boyfriend load. What I'm saying is, sometimes we try to fix things by adding something else. We say, I'm lonely, therefore I need a man/girl. I'm stressed therefore I need sex. The equation must be I have a problem, therefore, I go to Jesus to help me out. God will help you sort your loads correctly, and give you the right things to make them clean.

Just like the verse says, God will give you joy for your sorrow. You might have been sad because you feel like your life is a habitual mess, however, God will give you the joy that you have been looking for. God is the only one who can clean your mess. A man can't fix it, a new job can fix it, and a new woman can't fix it. God is the only one who can sort it out.

WEEK 46

A Time For Everything

"There is a time for everything, and a season for every activity under the heavens: a time to be born and a time to die, a time to plant and a time to uproot, a time to kill and a time to heal, a time to tear down and a time to build, a time to weep and a time to laugh, a time to mourn and a time to dance, a time to scatter stones and a time to gather them, a time to embrace and a time to refrain from embracing, a time to search and a time to give up, a time to keep and a time to throw away, a time to tear and a time to mend, a time to be silent and a time to speak, a time to love and a time to hate, a time for war and a time for peace."

Ecclesiastes 3:1-8

When you cut yourself, there is always a time where the cut will bleed. If you're dealing with a completely healthy person, the cut will stop bleeding eventually, and it will even stop hurting. There is a time when the bandage is on, and there is also a time where you must take the bandage off.

When we go through emotional hurt, sometimes we can rush people through the "getting over it" process. People will tell you, "Don't be sad," when you are crying. And they mean well, nobody likes to see a friend upset.

However, we must know that there is a time for everything! There is a time to cry. However, we also know that there is a time that we must laugh. There is a time where we will be happy and comforted.

If you feel like crying, cry! However, take your tears to the Father. Not to a significant other, not to your friends, take it to Jesus. God is close to the brokenhearted. He sees that you're hurt.

Now some might ask, "If there is a time to cry then why does it say in the Bible to rejoice in the Lord always?"

Notice, the verse says, rejoice in the LORD. This doesn't mean life is not going to get you down, but this does mean that you should find your gladness in God. The etymology of the word rejoice is actually to "enjoy the possession of". We must enjoy the possession of having Jesus! Even when stuff is bad, even when we are sad, there is still something to be encouraged about. Rejoice means to "be made glad". Be made glad that your heavenly Father loves you. Tears may endure for now, but trouble doesn't last. You might be sad now, but God will comfort you. Don't feel like you have to rush yourself. Don't feel like you have to immediately be happy, but always rejoice in the Lord. He is your strength in your weakness. Delight yourself in knowing that God loves you, and He sees the tears you have cried.

God understands how the loss of that loved one hurt. God understand how the death of that relationship stung. God knows! Just go to Him. His strength is made perfect in your weakness. Let the joy of the Lord be your strength.

WEEK 47

Don't Worry, God's Hovering

"In the beginning God created the heavens and the earth. Now the earth was formless and empty, darkness was over the surface of the deep, and the Spirit of God was hovering over the waters."

Genesis 1-2

There are times in life when it seems like nothing is happening. You are praying but for some reason, you feel like God is just not moving. You feel stuck. Nothing is moving forward or backward, it's just not moving at all.

When you are in seasons like this, it can get very hard to trust God. You can even get down on yourself and your own abilities. Of course, I will give you a small anecdote.

I remember I was installing a new software on my computer. I clicked on the link, and for some reasons, nothing popped up on my screen. I got frustrated thinking that my computer wasn't working. As I looked at the blank screen trying to decide what I was going to do, suddenly an icon showed up on my desktop to indicate that the software had finished downloading.

That's how God works. Think of the beginning of creation. The bible describes the world as dark, empty, and formless. However, when the world had no shape, no form, and no light, that was when God was hovering. Just like my software example, I couldn't see what was happening at the backend. I couldn't see that the software was downloading. Something was happening even though I wasn't physically witnessing it.

When your life seems to have no shape, no form, and no sense, that is when God hovers to make something happen. Take heart! Don't be discouraged. Things of eternity take time, but when they happen, they are worth the wait.

Some of you are in a situation that makes you wonder when God is going to move, however, know that He's already moving. Just because it's not physically being seen by you, does not mean that something is not being turned in heaven on your behalf.

Be encouraged. This season will be your testimony.

WEEK 48

Summertime In The Midst Of Winter

"A river watering the garden flowed from Eden; from there it was separated into four headwaters. The name of the first is the Pishon; it winds through the entire land of Havilah, where there is gold. 12 (The gold of that land is good; aromatic resin and onyx are also there.)"

Genesis 2: 10

I remember I visited California in the middle of the winter time. It was about 80 degree's and very sunny. My sisters and I had on shorts and skirts and flip-flops in the middle of the winter. In fact, some cities in the U.S. appear to be in a summertime season all the time, even though they are in the midst of fall or winter.

Why is it that these places like California and Florida are warmer in the winter months? Well, it's interesting to note that it has to do with the bodies of water that these areas are close to. These bodies of water, like the Gulf of Mexico and the Pacific Ocean, make the areas around them warmer.

Now, why are we talking about climate?

I say all of this to make a point. When you are surrounded by the right source of Water, you can experience summertime in the midst of your winter season. Meaning, when you are surrounded by Jesus, when you are in the cusp of God's hand, your wintertime and summertime can co-exist. Meaning it can TECHNICALLY be winter, but you can experience the summertime.

Going back to the verse, the word Pishon means to spring forth, it can also mean strength AND it can also mean rest. Havilah, which was the land close to the river Pishon means, "a circular writhing motion that can mean dancing or pain." When I looked at the verse I thought, those two things contradict each other! How can you have rest and spring forth, and how can you have something that denotes dancing or pain?

The verse tells us many things, and I'll explain them one at a time. Metaphorically speaking, if Jesus is the living water, and we are the land:

1. When you are close in proximity to the Water, or God, paradoxes can happen. Like summer in the winter time, or the ability to dance when you are in pain. Meaning although life can seem chaotic, you will have the peace that surpasses all men's understanding.

2. When God calls you to go forth to serve Him, you begin to abide in Him. And in Him, you will find rest. Even though you are springing forth, you will experience the rest of the Lord.

The point is, with Jesus, He can turn your mourning into dancing. He can turn your sorrow into joy. He can turn your loneliness into a relationship. He can turn your unemployment into a job. He can turn your application into acceptance. He can turn your lack into prosperity. In the meantime, however, if you stay close to the Savior, you can experience joy unspeakable despite your circumstance. You can experience ministry in the midst of your misery. You can experience pleasure in the midst of pain.

Lord, I pray for whoever is in a winter season that they feel won't come to an end. Help them to experience your summer Lord. Help them to encourage themselves by being encouraged through you. Lord, I really pray that you would help them see that their proximity to you is where they will find rest. In Jesus name,

Amen!

WEEK 49

Strength Training

"He gives strength to the weary and increases the power of the weak."
Isaiah 40:29

If you go to the gym every so often, you will have to up the intensity in order to get better results. I remember on one of my many runs at the gym, I decided to run an extra mile than I usually do to push myself a little harder. By the end of my workout I was in so much pain, and as I was leaving, one of the trainers yelled out, "Pain is weakness leaving the body!"

Without experiencing a little bit of pain, I would physically not be able to get stronger and stronger as I continue to work out. This is just like our Christian walk. You can't expect to grow if you never go through a little discomfort. If you never go through a little bit of pain, you will never gain wisdom that comes out of a bad situation.

Emotional pain can be spiritual weakness leaving out of your body. A bad breakup, a loss of a job, or even a financial hardship can leave you in a place where you have no choice but to have faith. These are the types of tests in lives that make us so much stronger. Just like working out, the pain will cease to exist when your muscles become strong enough to handle the weight. God is a good trainer. He will never let you max out on your weight. He will never let you hurt yourself to the point of destruction. However, He will allow a little bit of pressure to be put on you so that you can become the stronger man/woman that God has destined you to be.

Think about a time in your life that now looking back, you are smarter, wiser, and better. Also, God getting you through these trials increased your faith in Him. Another story is when I decided to get a trainer I was skeptical. I wondered if I could actually get results. I remember after the first session I was in so much pain that I was walking funny! But in a month's time, I started to see results, I started to trust my trainer more.

As you start to see yourself change, your character develops, your faith will become stronger. As you are faced with more difficult situations and are able to handle them with ease, your patience will become more fortified. However, all these things may come with waiting on God to give you a job, a mate, or a financial breakthrough. All these things will come with a bit of discomfort. Sometimes a lot of discomforts! But be encouraged, because this too shall pass. God is trying to take you to a higher level. Let him train you! The workout will never be easy, but you will become stronger.

Amen!

WEEK 50

When Bad Things Happen

Therefore, in order to keep me from becoming conceited, I was given a thorn in my flesh, a messenger of Satan, to torment me. Three times I pleaded with the Lord to take it away from me. But he said to me, "My grace is sufficient for you, for my power is made perfect in weakness." Therefore I will boast all the more gladly about my weaknesses, so that Christ's power may rest on me. That is why, for Christ's sake, I delight in weaknesses, in insults, in hardships, in persecutions, in difficulties. For when I am weak, then I am strong.

Corinthians 12: 7-10

Years ago a woman applied for a job that she was more than qualified for only to get rejected. She really wanted this job, so she continued to apply only to continue to get denial letters. A few months after, her rejection letters stopped. The company, Arthur Anderson, (firm involved in Enron scandal) was shut down because of fraudulent work practices.

Sometimes, bad things have to happen. We sit down and look at our lives and we wonder why God lets things happen to us. Reading about the Israelites and their quest to leave Egypt, during one of the plagues I noticed that the scripture said: "God hardened Pharaoh's heart towards them." (Exodus 10:27) When I read that, all I could think of was, God, didn't you want them to get out? Why didn't you make it easier by bringing Pharaoh down for the cause?

As Christians, we must realize that sometimes it is not the devil that is making things a little bit difficult. Sometimes God has a purpose for why something is a little bit harder than usual. Sometimes it might be that God is trying to protect you from something that you cannot see. Other times, it is because God is trying to teach us a lesson that will make us stronger. We must realize that bad things have to come and that with every cloud there is a silver lining. If the women in the story above, which happens to be my mother, would have worked for that accounting firm, her reputation would have been smeared.

Someone once told me that babies get sick a lot when they are young so that when they are older they are more immune to diseases. Sometimes in life, we have to get a little "sick" so that God can make us immune to bad situations.

With every bad thing that happens in your life, pain will come as well. However know that when God is putting you through something, there is a lesson that is to be learned out of it. We have to do our best not to miss the point. Don't miss the lesson that God is trying to teach you out of your pain. Don't let your labor go in vain.

It's not always going to be easy. God can't always give you the easy road because we would never learn anything. As you grow in your Christian walk, life tests will get harder and harder. Bad things will occur, but they are only there to teach you valid lessons you will need for the future.

They are only to prepare you for a greater destiny. Remember, you were built for the trails you face. All you have to do is trust God to sustain you and He will give you a helping hand.

WEEK 51

Stormy To Sunlight

"And provide for those who grieve in Zion— to bestow on them a crown of beauty instead of ashes, the oil of joy instead of mourning, and a garment of praise instead of a spirit of despair. They will be called oaks of righteousness, a planting of the Lord for the display of his splendor."

Isaiah 61:3

I remember one day I arrived at work right before some dark thick storm clouds hovered over the building. I rushed in to beat the rain, and right when I got to my desk I heard the loud rumble of thunder followed by an illuminating flash of lightening. It was about 9:00 am in the morning, but the sky was dark, so dark that it almost seemed like night. It was evident a storm was brewing. The rain started to come down in what seemed like sheets. It was coming down so hard, that it looked like it would never stop.

Storms like this happen in our lives. They hover over us and seem to be never ending. However, God sees the storm, and you can find refuge in Him! Just like I was able to get inside right before the storm hit, we can be sure that God will keep us safe in His arms even when the storms of life threaten to overtake us. Psalms 46:1 describes our God as a very present help in the time of trouble, and that he is our refuge. There is so much hope in that! We can always run to God for help, no matter what storm we face.

One hour later, the sun broke through, and suddenly it was very bright outside. I remember a couple hours later, it was as if it had never rained! The ground was dry, and there were no puddles or remnants of the storm that had passed. I took that as a direct word from God that although a person has gone through a storm, God can make it so that, when the storm passes, it will be as if it never hit.

I offer this word that God gave me to whoever is reading this. You may feel like you are in the middle of a storm. It may look like it will never be fixed. But God can calm whatever storm that is in your life. It may be a financial storm, a relationship storm or a family storm, however, whatever it may be, God has the power to turn it around. He has the power to make you change things. He will give you beauty for ashes. All you have to do is abide in Him.

WEEK 52

Lost And Found

Scripture Reading: Luke 15

While staying at a friend's house, I pulled out my necessary hair accessories to fix my mane. As I took strokes through the long tresses I noticed my hair was a bit dried out from the sun. I rummaged through my belongings and was able to find my one of my favorite hair dressings. I have many that I like, but this one smelled like coconut and sugar. I loved the way it made my hair feel. I put a dab in the palm of my hands and rubbed it gently in.

In a rush, while getting ready, I realized that I had lost the cap to my hair pomade. I looked all over the house and couldn't seem to find it. I looked for almost 2 hours because I did not want my little pomade to be thrown away.

This made me think of how the Lord thinks about us. In the story of the Prodigal Son in Luke 15, Jesus gives a parable of a son who had lost his way. What does it mean to be lost? The dictionary definition is to have gone astray. The son made many mistakes. The first being that he wanted a blessing prematurely. Getting a blessing before it is the right time can become a curse! He also was taking place in wild living, not following the right path.

Have you ever felt lost? Have you ever felt like you didn't know your way and you were just living from day to day aimlessly? Sometimes I've found when you finally realize you are lost, you feel like you can never go back to Jesus. You feel like you are so far gone that you can't go back to the Father.

One thing I noticed about the prodigal son story, is that when he finally realized that what he was doing wasn't working, he immediately assumed that he was no longer worthy to even be in his Father's house. This is a big lie from the devil. He makes you think that just because you have made a mistake that God will never accept you again! This isn't true.

The most beautiful part about the story is that the son was willing to take the least of what his Father had. But when he decided to turn around while he was still far off, his Father ran to him with open arms. God is just waiting for you to turn around. You don't have to have it all the right way. You don't have to be perfect; all you have to do is make a decision to turn in His direction.

God will take you back, and just like my lost cap to my pomade, He will seek you out! He won't let you go without a fight. God loves you that much, even when you don't deserve it. Even when you are wrong. Even when you are lost and you go astray. God still loves you anyway, and there is nothing—absolutely nothing that can separate us from that love.

If you are reading this, and you've been lost for a while and want to find Jesus, please pray the below prayer.

Dear Jesus,

I believe in you and I believe you have a plan for me. God I want to follow you. Lord forgive me of all my sins, and write my name in your Book of Life. I don't want to miss heaven.

In Jesus name Amen!

Made in the USA
Columbia, SC
03 August 2021